SINGLE *and* LOVING IT

how to be happy and whole when there is no other half

WENDY BRISTOW

Thorsons
An Imprint of HarperCollins*Publishers*
77–85 Fulham Palace Road,
Hammersmith, London W6 8JB

The Thorsons website address is: www.thorsons.com

Published by Thorsons in association with *Cosmopolitan* magazine 2000

3 5 7 9 10 8 6 4 2

A catalogue record for this book
is available from the British Library

ISBN 0 7225 4015 9

Printed and bound in Great Britain by
Caledonian International Book Manufacturing Ltd, Glasgow

Contents

Acknowledgements

A big thanks to Mandi Norwood for the lunch where we discussed the idea for this book and for making it possible. To Emma Dally for making it happen and to Carole Tonkinson for publishing it.

And to the women who shared their experiences of singlehood with me, especially:

Valentine Abbatt, Jan Ashford, Ramune Burns, Johanna Cruikshank, Sandra Donaldson, Emma Marlin, Maire Mayne, Anna Maxted, Sue Rickards, Marion Russell, Sasha Slater, Lou Trigg, Sue Wheeler. Plus Pam Bathe from Dateline, Emma Yablon and Matt Whyman from AOL and Philippa Perry.

And to everyone at Spectrum, especially Maggie McKenzie, Paul Allsop and Oriel Methuen, Terry Cooper, Jenner Roth and Rex Bradley, without whom I wouldn't know the first thing about many of the concepts in this book.

And to my book buddies, Ramune and Anna. Thanks.

Introduction

Right now I'm single when I never expected to be. As I write this, I am supposed to be in my happy-ever-after phase. Double dose. Because it was my second marriage which just went wrong only a year in, technically you could say I'm still supposed to be living out my first happy-ever-after too. But, as the Rolling Stones put it: you can't always get what you want (but if you try sometimes, you might get what you need). And being single does offer the opportunity to find out what it is we actually need, then learn to meet those needs ourselves.

The payoff is confidence, peace of mind and a sense of being in control of your destiny. And, ironically, being single and loving it makes you 10 times more attractive to the opposite sex. As one friend puts it, who after two years of grappling with singlehood suddenly finds herself swamped with interest just as she's set to fulfil a long-held dream of working abroad, 'There's nothing more alluring than someone who's happy with herself.'

This book is all about being a smug single: about becoming so happy with yourself that you're just as content and secure as when you're in a relationship. If not more so.

Whether singlehood was thrust upon you, or whether you chose it yourself. Whether you have children and a messy divorce and baroquely complicated access arrangements to negotiate, or whether you need never see your ex again. Whether you feel grief stricken about the end of your last relationship, or euphoric. Whether you've been single 10 years, or 10 minutes. Whether you couldn't care less if you never set eyes on another male again, or whether you're yearning for the real Mr Right. Whether your biological clock is going like a metronome, or whether it's broken down altogether. Whether you're a lone parent with one free night a week, or a woman-about-town with no strings ... Whoever you are, instead of seeing singleness as a curse or a failure, you can make it work for you. You can use it for a very specific purpose: to build and enhance your relationship with the one person who really matters: ***you.***

And, the magic payoff: all your relationships will blossom accordingly. When you know who ***you*** are and what ***you*** want, the whole business of relating to others becomes easier, less fraught.

This might be difficult to believe right now. We all arrive at singleness with either the baggage of a relationship gone wrong, or the burden of never having a relationship gone right.

That's why this book is written in three parts to reflect the three distinct phases of singledom: recovery from loss, learning to be alone and dating again. Not everyone goes about them in the same way. Some people go through all three stages while in a new relationship. Some do stage three first then visit the first two later on. Some pingpong around all three. It doesn't matter how you do it or in which order. What works is what works for you. You will be learning about yourself the whole time. Actually, the most important thing is not to judge yourself for the occasionally mad things you find yourself doing – and you will do mad things, that is all part of the process.

And, like me, you'll be learning all the time. This book is the sum total of what I've learnt about being single so far. I don't know all the answers. I do know what has worked for me and the women I've spoken to. I hope it works for you too.

CHAPTER 1

The Single Society

The fact more of us are single than ever before has social implications. Obviously housing is a big issue because there are more people on the market for housing. I think we'll see lots of changes in the kind of housing that's available to people.

Like where I live – an apartment complex in London which probably has 2,000 people living there and my guess would be the significant majority are single. It's interesting because there's a real single community there. It is one model of how the future could be.

I just got back from America, and certainly in the cities I felt completely relaxed going into a bar or a restaurant on my own because of the way they design things – there's always a bar where you can sit and be alone, you're not just stuck on a table feeling alone and vulnerable. Americans are much more at ease with single people, you don't feel a social pariah if you're on your own. And the US always hit the trends sooner than us.

Helen Wilkinson, single woman and project director at liberal think-tank Demos

However you arrived at singlehood, you may well be terrified.

I know a woman in a horrendous relationship with a womanizer and a drunk who gives as her only reason for staying: because I can't stand the idea of being alone on a Saturday night. Such is the fear of being single in our society that a statement like this may have many of us nodding sympathetically and breathing along with her: yes. Even while a part of us is screaming: *nooooooo.*

That 'no' is the healthy response. No relationship is better than a terrible relationship. Although the pain involved in facing up to the fact something isn't working – then often changing your life completely to reflect that fact – is understandably not something you leap into with abandon or with a tranquil heart.

Being single it's hard not to feel left out or, to use a horrible old phrase 'on the shelf'. Our society celebrates family values and sanctifies coupledom. From fairy stories to TV soaps we all love the happy ever after. But reality is not like that.

Reality Is Changing

In reality while the total adult population is projected to rise by 10 per cent between 1996 and 2021, the total number of single and divorced people will both increase by 50 per cent. At the same time, the married population will fall by about 10 per cent. As a result, married people will become a minority of the adult population by 2007. The number of people aged 35 to 44 who have never been married is projected to increase by 50 per cent between 2001 and 2011 and the number of single women aged 25 to 29 just about doubled between 1987 and 1997. (All according to recent figures from the Office of National Statistics.)

And with the divorce rate soaring and the boom in people cohabiting rather than marrying – an arrangement even easier to walk away from than marriage – the plain fact is that not only are we less likely to get married but we are also likely to be single more often in our lives.

It is no longer guaranteed that if we are in a relationship, if we marry even, we will never be single again. There is a high chance that we will be.

Helen Wilkinson is a project director at liberal think-tank Demos and spends her working life looking at trends. She believes there are several reasons why women are choosing to be single. She says:

One reason is the old gender contract has unravelled. The old contract traded economic independence for security in marriage. It's not holding women in the same way. Mainly because women now have more economic and cultural power. Therefore they have a greater ability to exit an unhappy relationship. It's significant the majority of divorces are initiated by women.

Then, because of these changes occurring, you're getting a culture in which people are more accepting about women being single. Indeed you could argue there's a whole popular culture around single women with Bridget Jones and Ally McBeal which, to an extent, even glamorizes that. You used to be on the shelf and that simply isn't the case any more.

So we had better get used to it!

Nonetheless, I have always arrived at singlehood with a heavy heart. (And I know I'm not alone. Dateline, the UK's biggest dating agency, estimate that 91 per cent of women – and 90 per cent of men – are looking for that one, special relationship.)

It's that feeling of: here we go again, back to square one, back on my own again, all that energy wasted, all that time wasted, all that ticking of the biological clock for nought. Time to dust myself off and start all over again. And I'm well aware that if children are involved, the situation is 10 times more painful and complicated.

Then you might start thinking: I have to be alone for a bit to recover from that relationship. I can't just launch into the next disaster (or I can, if I choose) but I do still need time to recover. At Relate they say it takes at least two years to recover from a serious relationship. And that in itself makes me angry.

Then you tell yourself: I have to date lots of men, probably (and if I'm lucky), before I meet the right one. Then spend time building a relationship with him. At this rate, I could be drawing my pension before I'm cosied up to Mr Right. Then there's that horrible nagging voice in my ear that taunts me with the fear I may never meet anyone ever again...

But. **STOP**. The whole point of this book is that being single need not be seen as some kind of a 'gap' before your life starts up again. It is genuinely a very enriching period in its own right.

I know this, because I have been single before. And because I've seen my girlfriends become single and grow dramatically during that time. Some have found an inner peace that always remained elusive when lurching from one relationship disaster to another.

Being single is a very specific set of circumstances with its own downside, setbacks and joys. Its own freedoms and blessings, triumphs and fulfillments. Eventually, for everyone, that initial sinking single feeling turns into a soaring single feeling.

This book is about getting to that soaring feeling as quickly as possible. It will allow you to explore your relationship with singledom – and offers a positive, specific programme for coping with the challenges of being on your own.

I hope you love it!

32 things that are great about being single

1. You can go to bed whenever you like
2. When you do go to bed, you can go *straight to sleep*
3. You can eat chocolate ice cream in bed without getting a mouthful of someone else's bellybutton fluff
4. You need never know how Man. U. are doing in the league
5. Christmas is cheaper
6. You can leave the flat trashed for two weeks and no one will call you a slut
7. Every time you answer the phone it's for you
8. So you can leave it to ring if you please
9. You get to see more of your girlfriends
10. You can flirt with the guy in the coffee shop guilt-free
11. Hell, you can flirt with the *girl* in the coffee shop guilt-free
12. There are never any black underpants greying up your whites wash
13. When friends moan about their men you can think: *Thank God*
14. You can stick to a diet – there's less temptation to eat pizza, drink lager, munch crisps
15. You can take control of the remote control
16. You can play with your friends' kids without complicating

the whole thing by demonstrating what a good *mother* you'd make

17 A vibrator never rolls over and falls asleep before you're finished

18 There's no one to say 'What did you do THAT for?'

19 You can watch a *Friends* video with no one complaining they're missing *Eurotrash*

20 You don't have to listen to the internecine politics of anyone else's office

21 You can stay in bed all day at the weekend with no one to say: Aren't you up yet?

22 If you choose, you can have a one-night stand, an affair – anything sexually thrilling, just for the sheer thrill of it

23 You don't have to spend hours with people you don't care about because they're *his* friends

24 You don't have to worry whether his mother likes you

25 You can tidy the flat – and it *stays* tidy

26 If the boiler busts, you get it fixed – there's no one saying I'll get around to it *next* weekend.

27 When you see an attractive woman, you don't have to wonder if he's spotted her too

28 You never have to think: Is this going anywhere?

29 You're not at the mercy of someone else's moods

30 There's never any bits of beard dotted round the sink

31 You can get a dog/cat/hamster and all future partners will just have to live with it

32 You can make that dream you've always had to write that novel/paint that painting/sail round the world a reality

11 things women love most about being single

When you're single the house stays tidy – if I don't make any mess, the house isn't messy, and if it is messy it's my mess and I know where it came from.

Alison, 29

You have far fewer responsibilities. I do feel you take on more responsibility in a relationship because you have someone else to worry about. OK, they're worrying about you too, which is great, but it's not always even. Women do tend to be the caretakers in relationships, emotionally and in other ways. I do think we end up doing more of the housework and chores so your responsibilities do increase.

Susan, 35

I'm always more independent when I'm single, and being independent is a good thing for me. To take a silly example, I learnt how to programme the video. When there's stuff needs doing that men would normally do, and you do it, you feel so good about it. But when he's around you let it slide, and soon not being independent becomes dependent...

Rachel, 27

I so love going out on those girly nights where anything could happen – then next morning you and your girlfriend pore over every detail, even when nothing much actually *did* happen.

Louise, 24

I love that feeling of possibility when you meet someone – when you sing all those songs in your head, you predict it all into the future. In a relationship, you can think, Oh, is this it then? I'll never have that wonderful excitement again.

Maire, 22

You get lazier in a relationship. It's very easy to stay in and watch television, which is a supremely unfulfilling pastime. When I was single I did go out a lot more – I think that's pretty universal.

Anne, 27

I love having my own time and space. I really like living alone and being alone when and if I choose. Sometimes I have a whole weekend where I just feel like time goes on forever – when I do what want when I want, I might even stay in my pyjamas all day. In theory living with someone shouldn't change that, but for me it does. Even having a great long bath with a magazine is different somehow when you live alone. It's that notion of pleasing only yourself, of not being accountable at all. It's what scares you the most about being single at first and the thing that's wonderful in the end.

Ria, 31

I love that feeling of knowing where I'm going because it's in my control. When someone comes into your life it's more uncertain, really. But when you've been single a while you really know that whatever happens you're going to survive. And that makes me feel good and strong.

Sue, 36

It's wonderful being able to do anything, anything at all. Not having to always think about another person and whether you can do it or not. I like that. I've probably travelled more in the last three years while I've been single than I've done in my lifetime. I've been away three or four times a year. If a friend says: let's go to Portugal, I can just drop everything and go. Whereas in a relationship you think: I've only got four weeks holiday and I'd better spend it with him...

Sarah, 34

One of the great things about being single for a while is that you realize you don't actually *need* anyone, so when someone comes along it's a nice, relaxed feeling, not that horrible I won't survive otherwise kind of way. That's crucial.

Ria, 31

The best thing about being single is making decisions just for you. The freedom of knowing you can do exactly what you want. Even little things like you can lie in bed and do a starfish just because you can and think, ooh this is great. But you can also go and live in Australia for a year if you get the chance. That feeling of freedom is very special.

Kate, 30

See. It's not so bad after all. But often we can't come to appreciate the good stuff because of all the hurt that's in the way. Which leads us to...

PART ONE

Achieving an Ending

It may be that you're totally ecstatic at being a solo flyer, couldn't care less about your ex – or don't have an ex – and can't wait to bite the dating bullet. In which case, skip this next bit and go on to part three.

If you're bursting into tears every 10 minutes, still have up and down days and never quite know which it's going to be today, then you *know* you're not over him yet. Read on, and you soon will be...

CHAPTER 2

Ending the Blame Game

Your quality of singleness depends such a lot on how you break up with your last relationship. For me, that was very difficult because I had so much bitterness to deal with. In my case, my ex said he absolutely loved me, he just wanted sex with this other woman. And in theory that shouldn't have been any big number but it was. It's still a betrayal. So I had to deal not just with being single but with being betrayed. And what it brought up in me was ug-ly.

Had it been more amicable I wouldn't have felt so dirty and used and angry and I wouldn't have gone to such dark places as I did. But I'm grateful for them now, I feel like I linked in to a part of me that's dark and horrible and it's useful to know she's there. But I couldn't step straight into a sense of abundant singleness because I felt so wretched.

Sarah, 35, three years after the breakup of her relationship

Indeed.

The one crucial factor for enjoying a successful singlehood with any hope of positivity is to deal effectively with the ending of your last relationship. If it ended amicably and you sail into singlehood filled with relief and possessed of a certainty it would never have worked out, congratulations.

You can skip this next part. But if you have any squeak of doubt, any twinges of guilt; if you have any clutches of wild, raging fury; if you find yourself suddenly stopped in your tracks by nostalgia when passing the restaurant you went to on your first date ... then read on.

You can tell when people haven't achieved 'closure', as the Americans put it. Months, even years down the track, an evening out with them turns into a moan-fest about how appalling their ex is, how unattractive his latest girlfriend is, how poky his new flat is, how ridiculously penis-like his latest car is. They make it their business to be incredibly well-informed about what he's up to now – and what he's up to now is always a long litany of crimes and misdemeanours. On this one subject their manner suddenly becomes extremely animated. Their voice is louder, their body perks up. They go on. They do not know when to stop. They blame as though they had taken out the patent on blaming. Yet if you say to them: You're not over him yet, they will retort something along the lines of: The hell I am.

If you have a sneaking suspicion this might be you, bear in mind it is not good. For two reasons:

It keeps you stuck

Friends eventually get bored at your lack of moving on-ness and lose patience.

Yet immediately after the break-up of any relationship you need to talk. And talk. And talk some more. You need to vent all those feelings of guilt or revenge. You need to go over it again and again with different people trying to make sense of it, even if it just doesn't make sense and never will do.

Just quit the blaming.

Save yourself months in therapy and take it from me: if you're stuck blaming him you'd be better off – and healthier – taking all that focus and turning it on yourself. And no, this does not mean blaming yourself. But putting all that blaming *energy* on yourself. This could be tricky: it means taking responsibility for your life, it means looking at your own patterns. But I promise it will make you feel better 10 times quicker. And by taking responsibility for your own life and happiness you stand a far better chance of making happiness a reality in your future.

After my first husband left I became obsessed by how appalling his behaviour was ... and it was. But now I realize he was doing his best and probably intended no malice. I just couldn't bear my feelings of rejection and abandonment. I wanted people to believe he was terrible so I wouldn't have to face a sneaking suspicion I was, or why would he have left?

The fact is, I *was* a victim. I had no idea about strategies to get rid of me that were going on behind my back. A thief in the night came and took everything I held dear.

I needed to talk it out. I needed to kick his most expensive shirt all round the house. I needed to indulge horrid fantasies of letting the tyres down on his bright new sportscar.

But there comes a time to let go. I knew I had to stop when a counsellor told me I could whinge for Europe in the world whinging championships.

The minute you stop focussing on *him* you learn so much more about you. And learning about yourself is one of the wonderful payoffs of singlehood. Learn about yourself and you need never be the same again. And that's a first, powerful step in making sure total relationships disaster never happens to you again.

And yes, his behaviour may well have been truly awful. But if you want to get even, happiness is the best revenge. And you'll never get there while you're stuck in the 'poor me' corner feeling sorry for yourself. I'm not suggesting you shouldn't feel horrible feelings. Just recognize them for what they are and focus on the only person who really matters, the only person you can do anything about: ***you***.

As Sarah, whose voice began this chapter, puts it:

I found out my mum was dying, then my partner met someone else and wanted the break-up to be easier than it was. I was dealing with his naffness over and over again. That was when I thought this is just crazy. Let him do whatever he has to do, but stop putting all your attention on him. Stop it. And it was a marathon. Everyday – focussing, focussing, take the focus off that relationship, off that relationship. That was the beginning of being single. I thought, I get one shot of being with mum while she dies so I'm not going to focus on him. And it was a daily, daily thing, renewing my effort and my focus.

In some funny way it almost helped, mum dying. I thought how long am I going to carry on dragging out the death of this relationship when in fact I've got someone dying right in front of me. It helped me get clearer that I can't spend that energy there.

Checklist

Subtle signs you're not over him

Blaming/ranting
Feeling fury when anyone mentions him
Feeling fury around anything you have to do to adapt your life without him
Finding yourself driving past his office/house/gym/whatever
Finding yourself *avoiding* driving past his office/home/gym/whatever
Feeling a charge when you speak of him, getting wound up, voice louder, speech faster
Feeling fury when people say it'll take time
Constantly distracting yourself from thinking/feeling about him with food, alchohol, work etc

If you're still not convinced about this blaming business, take a tip from the US queen of self-help, Susan Jeffers, author of the self-explanatory *Feel the Fear and Do It Anyway*. She says:

The underlying payoff of all 'victim' excuses, of course, is that by staying 'stuck', we don't have to push through the fear and take responsibility for our lives. We don't have to pull ourselves out of the muck and mire. We can just sit there and play the role of victim.

You might be asking 'Why don't I just stay in a state of blame? It sure is easier that way.' My answer is that there are many good reasons for giving up the payoffs and honouring who you are as a human being. A few of those reasons are: happiness, peace of mind, satisfaction, joy, self-respect, confidence, a life well lived.

Get the focus on you

Now that's out of the way, the second most important thing to remember is: be gentle with yourself. Treat yourself like a best best friend. You've been through a hell of a thing, often compared with bereavement. But which can feel even worse because the person isn't dead, they're still around and quite possibly sleeping with your best friend.

Experts vary in their estimates of how long it takes to recover from the ending of a significant relationship. Some say minimum six months; Relate, the marriage guidance organization say two years. The women I spoke to for this book varied enormously, but the estimates tended to be years not months.

This may well fill you with horror. And fury. It did me. Ditto my friend Jacqui who says:

*I remember when I first split up with my ex people said it's going to take you a year to get over him and I thought F*** that! No way is that man going to make me waste a year of my life getting over him. I was really angry. Little did I know it was actually going to stretch to three years. Not in the same degree of intensity as at the beginning, but it does take time.*

The good news – impossible though it may be to believe that there is any good news when your life, your wishes, hopes and dreams have just gone the way of the Beatles after Yoko – is you can speed up the process. The not-so-good news is that you do this by really facing up to the pain.

And facing up to the pain means...

CHAPTER 3

Dealing with the Feelings

Right now I'm never sure how I'm going to be from one day to the next. One day I'll be completely fine, the next I'll wake in a fury and be furious all day. Or I'll wake depressed and that turns into a fury by teatime. Or I'll wake fine and a little thing will trigger me off and I'll be weepy all day. Some days I feel I experience every emotion known to woman, plus a few I made up myself! All I can say is, gradually, I'm having more good days than bad.

Rosa, 29, five months after the break-up of her marriage

Not again.
But I thought that was it!
But he said he'd always love me.
But he's the father of my kids.
Now what?
What if I never find anyone again?????

Feelings have a purpose. They are signals. Feelings are like the man who comes to read the gas meter – they just need attending to and then they'll go away. Ignore them, and, like the man from the gas board, they'll keep coming and bugging you until you learn to read your own emotional meters.

Emotions hold the key to healing. I wish I'd known this when my first relationship broke up. I was instantly obsessed with 'why'. Why did he leave? What was really going on for him and why didn't he tell me? Why her? Why now? Why, why, *why*? I would lie awake trying to understand it in my head. I would puzzle it out to friends. I would ask him – why? And it was one question he wouldn't, probably couldn't, answer. With the wisdom of hindsight I realize I could have helped myself no end by letting go of the why and having a good cry.

A very wise man I once met, who worked as a healer, said 'God gave us the heart to live by and the head to understand the heart's feelings. Not the other way around.'

Feelings are important. Feelings matter. We live in a society which treats emotions like it treats the homeless – ignore them and maybe they'll go away. It's like we British, with our stiff upper lip, are allergic to feelings, so determinedly do we tend to negate them. With the best will in the world, friends and family can try and block them with messages like: 'Don't cry', 'He's not worth getting this worked up about', 'You should be over this by now', 'Calm down'. They mean well, but ignore them. Your feelings are your best friends. You need them around.

Moreover, we all have our own personal likes and dislikes where emotions are concerned; certain feelings we're better with than others. You might cry like a tap but never let yourself be angry. Or you might be filled with righteous indignation, but never allow softer feelings like sadness. Or your focus might all be on jealousy and obsessing about the fat blonde your ex flew off with. Yet all emotions are natural. And when they pass through us, that's how they pass.

Why do emotions get such a bad press? One obvious reason: they're painful. Plus we're trained to vent or repress certain emotions from our childhood. To take an extreme example, if your father was violent, you're going to fear violent rage ebbing up in you. If your best friend's father was violent, she's going to fear anger ebbing up in you. Yet all emotions are natural, and you're going to feel all of them after a breakup.

Think about babies. They howl when they're upset and gurgle when they're happy. And scream when they're angry or really hurting. They haven't yet learnt to 'control themselves'. But that way, they also get it all out. Babies don't hold grudges. You need to be a baby for a little while and get it all out.

It may feel scary. You may hate the idea of feeling. As Rosa says, 'I can't bear being like this. My life has been fine up to now and suddenly, boom, it all falls apart and I literally have no experience like this to match it against. I feel I've lost control.'

This is a common fear, but actually, emotions never truly overwhelm us. They're more likely to turn into problems like depression when we repress them, not express them. The way to deal with them is feel them, not let them fester.

I didn't understand this six years ago when my first marriage broke up, and I didn't really deal with my feelings of grief, rage and impotence. And look what happened. Now I can see that many of my actions of the past six years can be viewed as a kind of compensation, a distraction from the incredible pain created by being left by the man I'd shared every day with for 10 years.

Defence Mechanisms

Because some feelings can be so incredibly painful, we all have defences we use unconsciously to protect ourselves.

So we eat too much, or fling ourselves into another relationship, or go mad clubbing and behaving badly or go out and screw every man we see. Or, most commonly, we 'get on with it'. If all your friends compliment you on how well you're coping, do let the compliment seep in, but also, when you're home alone, just question yourself as to make sure you're not just in toy soldier mode.

And, yes, what you're defending against can be truly awful. You feel like you're dying, like you can't go on, like it's all too much, it's awful to feel this way, isolated in your pain, words like 'desperate', 'despairing' suddenly are no longer words in a dictionary, but part of your day.

In short, it's horrible. But...

Often what we're defending ourselves against feeling doesn't feel as bad as we fear it will.

Distraction mechanisms for running away from feelings:

Drinking too much
Having sex
Flirting
Working too hard
Compulsive overeating
Going out too much
Throwing yourself into the lives of your children/ focussing on them
Denial – it doesn't hurt too much
Throwing yourself into another relationship
Watching TV all the time
Obsessively dieting
Obsessively exercising

Exercise

Sit and sense your current emotional weather. Is there any pain around? Any loneliness? Or do you feel OK? If there is any hurt, just try and sense it and say to yourself 'What if it's OK to feel like this?'

Try doing this for 10 minutes a day. And for moments throughout the day, ask 'What am I feeling now?' when people you trust ask you how you are, try saying, 'today I'm sad' rather than always answering in a knee-jerk way 'I'm OK'.

This is what author of the best-selling women's self-help book *Women Who Love Too Much* Robin Norwood calls 'holding still' with the feelings. Not running away from them. Not distracting from them, but holding still until they pass.

Also, remember there's a relationship between thoughts and feelings. At this time you need to think positively and not have thoughts that contribute to your lows, but that build up your highs. (There will be more on this in Chapter 4.)

Learning To Manage Your Emotions – What To Do

Remember the worst possible thing you can do in the wake of a break-up is repress your feelings. Emotions do pass if you recognize them and speak them. So, call a friend and say, I feel sad today, or I'm angry. If they're not in, say it to their answering machine. If that's impossible, just acknowledge it to yourself. Forget all that stuff about the first sign of madness being talking to yourself. Say out loud to yourself: I'm sad.

Feelings journal

An incredibly powerful healing tool is already in your hands which costs no more than the price of a biro and a piece of paper. It's called writing.

The sheer simplicity of putting feelings down on paper has benefits out of proportion to the act itself. A researcher on writing therapy, J. W. Pennebaker, professor of psychology at the Southern Methodist University in Dallas, has monitored the relationship between writing and feelings and made powerful discoveries. In one test he asked a group to write for 20 minutes about their life's most disturbing experiences, while a control group wrote about mundane subjects, like what they did on their holidays. He found the first group's health was much better over a six-month period, with fewer visits to the doctor. He also asked unemployed professionals to write out their deepest feelings about losing their jobs, and compared them with a similar group who wrote about everyday, non-emotional matters, and found the first group were not only happier and healthier, they found jobs much more quickly.

Writing works then. Here's how to make it work for you.

Keep a feelings journal, your own private place where you pour out all your feelings about your break up, your ex, being single. No one else needs to read it, so you can be as bitchy, snide or plain despairing as you want. Let your journal be your best friend, where you confess thoughts and feelings even your real best friend doesn't know about. Do it every day and you'll be putting in time with yourself, for yourself.

One tip: Try not to end on a downer, but do your best to write yourself into a more positive frame of mind. You could write positive affirmations at the end of each daily session (there's more on affirmations in Chapter 12).

And try to write something each day, or as often as possible.

Apart from making you feel better right now, a positive side-benefit is that in the future you will be able to look back to how you were, the thoughts you were thinking, the emotions you were feeling and note your progress. (And, yes, there will *be* progress.)

And who knows, generations from now some descendant of yours may find it in an attic and it may help *them* through a break-up.

If writing's just not your thing, you could try drawing pictures of how you feel. They don't have to be artistic or good, they're for you, to get the feelings out. They can look like a child's drawing; or they may be abstract blobs. As long as they mean something to you. You really can transform things through art.

If you're feeling run down or about to explode with the demands of trying to cope, you could try going away for a week alone. I did this several times while my second marriage was dissolving, and it did me no end of good. I found a lovely woman who had a sweet little coastguard's cottage to rent which became my sanctuary. No demands, no pressures. Just me, the sea and a very large box of tissues.

When The Feelings Become Too Much

Practical tips that help

I had a Café Lonely phase. There was a little Italian café round the corner from me and I'd take my washing to the launderette, then sit in what I called my Café Lonely and have a café latte and reflect how no man was appreciating my wonderfulness. I'd go when I was particularly sad, but it got to the point where I'd sit there and think how wonderful it was to be so sad and reflect. It was my own little ritual that was designed to make me feel better and in the end was one of the things I most miss about being single.

Ella, 26

Sadness

Everything reminds you of him. Certain places remind you of him, certain songs remind you of him, even certain foods remind you of him. And a pang of sadness hits you every time you are reminded. After I broke up with my first husband, I realized with a horrid shock that everything which had happened in an entire *decade* reminded me of him – everything from Margaret Thatcher to posh cheese.

Then there are all the plans you had. The wishes, hopes and dreams. Who will I go on holiday with now? Who will I spend my Sundays with now? Who will take me out on my birthday now?

Sadness and, at its more extreme, grief, are seen as the feminine emotions. We're almost expected to feel them. Which doesn't, frankly, make them any easier. Here are some pointers for easing your grief…

- Be really gentle with yourself. Allow your grief. And remember that in this state you feel very vulnerable.
- There's a common fear which goes: 'if I allowed myself to start crying, I'd never stop'. Do not scare yourself with this. It is not true. I allow my grief nowadays and the longest I've ever cried is on and off for a few hours. And I didn't die, and I stopped. And the next day I woke up feeling much better.
- Try indulging your sadness, just for a bit, to get it out: listen to sad songs, watch a weepy movie, write a poem, put a sad song on the stereo and dance a sad dance.

- Try and avoid sentimental over-dramatizing along the lines of 'I'll never be able to enjoy a sunset ever again'.
- Have a 'duvet day'. If you wake up and really feel you can't get up, don't.

10 songs to listen to when miserable (to make you even more miserable)

You could even make your own grief tape for when you need a howl/to feel thoroughly sorry for yourself.

'I can't make you love me' – George Michael
'You have been loved' – George Michael
(in fact anything slow by latter-day George Michael)
'Walking Wounded' – Everything But the Girl – (in fact, the whole album, *Do you like being single?*)
'Missing' – Everything But The Girl
'Music Sounds Better With You' – Stardust
'Tears of a clown' – Smokey Robinson
'How can you mend a broken heart?' – Al Green
'Without You' – Mariah Carey or Nilsson
'Layla' – Eric Clapton (I know it's about his loving a woman, but so what)

Anger...

...an emotion 'nice girls' don't feel. But, contrary to the messages we often get growing up, it's good to get angry. It's healthy and necessary and does us more harm when we hold it in.

Again, as with tears, we can fear that if we give vent to our anger we'll lose control, hit someone, or simply explode. And again, this will not happen as long as you understand that you *can* control your anger, so it is not controlling you.

Plus anger makes you feel good and strong. It pumps your body full of adrenalin so you get high for a while on your own chemicals.

Anger pointers...

- Anger invites action. So get it out by doing something physical – punching cushions is a good one, or going for a jog where every step you envisage stomping on your ex's face (ugh!), or take it out on the equipment at the gym. Making noises is good – sitting in your car with the windows up, screaming your head off. Growling into a pillow – whatever gets you through the angry night.
- Write your ex a letter you never send. Tell him/her all the angry thoughts, bitterness, resentments. Tell him/her the consequences of their bad behaviour in exquisite detail. Tell him/her what you'd love to do to them. Then burn it. It can be immensely satisfying to watch your angry words go up in smoke.
- Indulge a few violent fantasies. Psychologists believe violent fantasies are very useful in venting violent feelings. They point to how children have no qualms about voicing their horrid thoughts of what they'd like to do

to little Johnny who stole their toy bus. Violent fantasies can be useful, *as long as you're clear you're* not *actually going to send the boys round or slash his tyres.*

- Sit in a chair, visualize him sitting in a chair in front of you and talk your anger out.

A word about vindictiveness. Act it out if you must, but it only makes you look, and feel, smaller. I really believe you block *yourself* when your inability to let go means you act out your aggression. You feel bad enough already, without giving yourself more to feel bad about.

Jealousy

A horrid emotional state to be in, jealousy is actually a secondary emotion which often hides a masked feeling.

It is desire turned inside out. The experts say if you follow envy or jealousy back to its source you'll always find something that needs fixing, some need that's unmet, some ambition thwarted, some insecurity that needs a confidence-booster. I'm sure, post-break-up, you don't have to be Freud to find the root of your jealousy.

Jealousy pointers...

- Ask yourself what is it I actually want? If you're envious of your ex's new woman it's obviously because she has what you want: him. So mourn your loss. Admit to yourself how much you miss him, rather than focussing on negative resentment of *her*. And remember, she did not steal him, he went. The responsibility always lies with the person who has the affair. Perhaps you find yourself envying people with seemingly perfect lives, a common reaction to the chaos you find yourself in After The End. So, again, focus on the positive. Ask yourself how you're going to get the life you want now (exercises in part two will help you)

- As with anger, write a letter you never send.
- Remind yourself what you have. And if you can't think of anything, freedom is a good place to start.
- Don't allow yourself to get bitter. He's not worth it. No one's worth it.

Depression

Depression, characterized by low energy, listlessness, a sense of 'what's the point?', is actually a non-emotion and often has a real but suppressed emotional state behind it. Many experts believe depression is anger turned inward on yourself which sets up a 'what's the point' attitude. Or it's a numb form of grief.

Depression pointers...

- Ask yourself: am I really angry? Often when people say they'd love to cry but can't, it's because they're actually angry. Or numb. Numb can be an emotional state too.
- If symptoms persist – that is, if you find yourself in a state of depression for several weeks, or feel unable to

cope – it is a good idea to go see your GP and talk it over with him. He may refer you for counselling, or give you a mild antidepressant that will tide you over until you feel better.

Fear

You thought you had everything sorted. You thought everything was just fine. And now it's not. Now it's very much not.

And it's totally understandable that you should be afraid.

It could be said that all negative emotions – jealousy, anger, guilt – stem from fear. And fear begins in our own mind, from hanging on to the past and trying to manage the future already. So we fuel the fearful fire with thoughts like: How will I handle my life now. This is terrible. I can't cope. Plus, of course, the number one fear of all the women I spoke to: ***what if I never find anyone ever again???*** (*see box on page 39*)

Fear pointers…

- Breathe. When we're frightened our breathing becomes rapid and shallow. It is very difficult to breathe deeply and feel fear at the same time.
- Phone a friend. Talk your fears over with them and let them reassure you everything will be all right.
- In your journal, list your fears about being single. Like: I'll never find love again; What if he was 'The One' and

I'll never find another? I'll never manage alone; I won't have enough money to pay the mortgage etc.; What if his lawyers shaft me and I'm left with nothing? There's something comforting about anchoring fear thoughts down.

- Use the phrase from the scared-person's bible *Feel The Fear And Do It Anyway* and tell yourself: Whatever happens, I'll handle it. And know that you will.
- If you're having panic attacks, see your doctor.

The single woman's number one fear:
'What if I never find anyone?'

Again and again, for the women I talked to, this was the number one bugbear. The scary little thought that would enter their heads last thing at night; the gremlin lurking behind all manner of strange behaviours, unfeasible dates, down days and sudden temper tantrums.

It underlies many of our actions. Like blaming. If it's his fault then it can't be our fault. Because if it was our fault there might be something wrong with us, and if there's something wrong with you, you might *never find anyone*. Or flirting with the acne-ridden teenager in the post room just because he's male and he's giving you the eye and he might be your last ever chance because you *might never find anyone*.

This is, of course, faulty thinking. Or, as the shrinks would have it, 'catastrophic thinking'.

Either way, it doesn't do you any good.

You need to think positive to counteract it.

One of the best cures for catastrophic thinking is to look the catastrophe hard in the eye and tell yourself:

Even if I never find anyone, I will still be OK. I won't die. I might have a different life than if I find someone, but I'll still be alive and being alive offers many things to enjoy. I'll still have my dog, house, children/whatever. There will still be great films to see, books to read, places to visit, friends to love.

Or whatever vision of living with the worst that could happen works for you.

Other things you can do to support yourself:

Make affirmations (*see page 160*) like, 'I am attracting a wonderful relationship into my life'.

Have a friend you call when you're having a *What if I never find anyone?* moment. Tell her her job is to reassure you: there are actually loads of men out there; you're a wonderful woman; there's someone for everyone etc...

Think of all the women you know who, against the odds, hooked up with someone. Ask yourself if you're truly ready. When you're not really ready you don't give off come-and-get-me-vibes. Then, one day, something changes and men are like London buses, several come at once.

Remember your life is not on hold until you meet him. Every time you have a *what if...?* panic, do something for you. Buy yourself a book, go for a walk, arrange a girl's night, call a dating agency, whatever will get you out of the WIINFA? hole.

Guilt

Maybe you ended it and he's heartbroken. Maybe you had an affair and you feel bad about that. Maybe there are children involved and they're unhappy.

Maybe all the starving children in the Third World would not go hungry if only you'd done something differently.

Maybe you indulge in faulty thinking, like if only I hadn't nagged him/worn those grey old knickers/worked so hard and spent more time with him, it would have worked.

Stop it. Now. This is guilt, and guilt *always* has a critical thought behind it. Moreover, it always creates self-punishment. And don't you feel bad enough already? When you punish yourself, you feel even worse guilt, so you punish yourself some more and get caught in a downward spiral which can exaggerate a crisis into a tragedy.

You did the best you could, just as we are all doing the best we can all of the time. Even when we're not doing the best we can, we're doing the best we can, if you see what I mean.

Guilt pointers...

- To come over all new-agey for a minute, you have to forgive yourself. You can't change anything about the past. You can only change how you feel about it now. After my second marriage ended I nearly drove myself mad with – did I do the right thing? In the right way? For the right reasons? And what I learnt eventually was one of the most valuable lessons of my life: that all is fair in love and war. There are no rules. And maybe I just made a mistake.

- If you had an affair, bear in mind that while 83 per cent of the population think that 'extra marital affairs are always or almost always wrong', society is now more adulterous than ever before. For obvious reasons, it has been hard for researchers to find out exactly how many people have sex outside a committed relationship but in their book *Sexual Arrangements* (William Heinemann Ltd.), relationships experts Janet Reibstein and Martin Richards estimate that between half and 75 per cent of married men and only a slightly lesser proportion of married women have had affairs.
- Guilt does not allow for correction, only punishment. Look at your situation neutrally, if you can, see what the mistake was and correct the mistake, if you can. If you can't, promise to learn from it and not make the same mistake again.
- Make amends to anyone you can that you feel really bad about. Write them a letter, drop them a note saying 'sorry'. You'll immediately feel better, and so might they.
- Don't get caught up in over-compensation. Guilt can prompt us to fall over backwards trying to please

people we feel guilty towards – our children, our ex. And in the process, we lose ourselves.

With every emotion, keep asking yourself: What if it's OK for me to feel like this?

Phew! Going through all this, expect to feel tired. All this grieving, shock, anger, jealousy takes up energy and you may well feel more tired than usual. Be gentle with yourself. You may need to sleep more.

What you can look forward to...

If you ended it...

There'll be guilt, regret, doubt. Even if you're a ball of fury for weeks there may well be a time when grief and self-doubt set in. If only for 10 minutes.

If he ended it...

You'll be in shock for a while, even if you were half expecting it. Then, likely as not, you'll go through fury, revenge, depression...

If it was a marriage...

The stakes are very high, after that glittering ceremony where you promised one another commitment. Then there's the end of all those wishes, hopes and dreams; the sense of certainty and security that it would last. Not to mention the whole palaver of divorce and dealing with lawyers.

If there are children...
Everything becomes massively more complicated. Despair, guilt, anger at him/whoever for not making it work for their sake. Plus the fact that you will always have to have some contact with one another for the children's sake.

If money was involved...
And it so often is. Ivana Trump and Larry Fortensky have not been the only two people to attempt to get their exes to pay for their pain. Finances and heartbreak tend to be a lethal combination sparking intense fear (of loss, of poverty), the desire to win, and revenge.

If friends are involved...
Whether he's gone off with one, you've gone off with one, or friends have ganged up against one or other partner, the sense of betrayal can be astronomical (*see Chapter 6*, page 72, for more on how friendships change when you become single).

So much for emotions, but the heart and mind are not two separate things, they're connected up in this thing we have called a body. Hence there are ways of thinking which can make the feelings worse...

CHAPTER 4

Listen to Yourself

When Ben left, I was at my wit's end. I couldn't seem to get over it. Eventually, I went to see a counsellor. She pointed out to me how I was being really hard on myself. That I was beating myself up and judging myself and blaming myself and she said how that can make it take longer. I don't do it half so much now and, not only has it helped me get over him, it's helped me feel a whole lot better about myself in all walks of life.

Rosa, on how faulty thinking was preventing her recovering from break-up

Of course, feelings don't happen in isolation. They go hand in hand with our thoughts. Thoughts create feelings and, often, vice versa.

When you're recovering from a relationship that didn't work out there are three sorts of thought channels that aren't helpful. One is obsessing on him in an 'if only...' kind of way. (Or a 'that bastard...' kind of way.) Two is scaring yourself. The other is beating yourself up.

Your thoughts don't just happen. Your mind isn't a continual circus that happens inside your head. Yet it is the nature of the mind to think. And once you become aware of it, you can choose your thoughts. There are thoughts which perpetuate the cracks and melt the glue; there are thoughts which speed up the mending process. The exciting thing is, this is something you can do every day, every minute as a way of taking control, making yourself feel better, recovering, mending your broken heart.

Without any awareness of how your mind is trying to deal with the pain of break-up, more often than not, it creates thoughts which are a complete – and effective – distraction.

Obsessing

I realized the other day that, when I have nothing else to think about, my thoughts go back to him again and again. And they only always go back to the good times. The sweet, happy times (not the times he was in a bad mood), the great sex (not the times he couldn't get it up), the laughter and companionship (not the times when he wouldn't speak to me, not the times he shouted at me). And never the times I felt lonely and exhausted or angry and frustrated and wondered what was the point of all this hassle. When I notice this, I have to consciously run another think-tape!

Maria, 25, on obsession

Immediately after my rebound relationship ended I sat down and added up the unpleasant incidents I'd experienced and they were exactly equal to the good times – one shitty weekend for every lovely walk in the country; one time when he wouldn't talk to me for every time he was lovely and funny and sweet; one horrible row for every time he brought me flowers (in fact, thinking about it, the flowers always came *after* the horrible rows).

But another part of me could be just like Maria and watch myself going back to the good times, obsessing on the lovely things when if I focussed on the horrible things I didn't have to put up with anymore I might have an opportunity to feel differently about my single status.

And when I did, I did.

Maybe you're obsessing about someone you fancy. Or your ex. Or food. Whatever it is, **it's OK. Just notice you are obsessing.**

Maybe you're not obsessing at all, in which case, well done. In the wake of trauma, obsessing is a very common defence mechanism. It protects us from the very painful feelings we'd have to think about if we weren't obsessing on something outside ourselves.

Beating Yourself Up

There is, in all of us, a little voice that constantly tells us off. Psychologists and psychotherapists have given this voice various names, including 'critical voice', 'inner critic', 'the chatterbox', 'top dog', 'the monkey mind'.

Whatever you call it, you've got one. It's likely it sounds like one of your parents, or an old schoolteacher. Or it might sound like a part of you you created all by yourself and doesn't reflect anyone or anything.

This voice doesn't let you get away with a thing. Whatever you do it finds something to criticize you for. It plants doubts, even about things you feel are right. It questions, it criticizes. It nags. It says things like:

You're too fat, you're crap at relationships, you're too old, you're too needy, you're a wreck.

It uses words like 'should' and 'ought' a lot, as in:

- You should have been more affectionate – if you had been he'd never have left
- You should have been more sexy
- You should never have gone off sex
- You should have been more angry instead of bottling it up
- You should have been less demanding
- You shouldn't be feeling like this – after all, you ended it
- You ought not to be still feeling like this, he's been gone three months
- You ought to be over this by now

- You ought to be working, not mooning over some bloke
- You ought not to go out with anyone else right now
- You ought to be nicer to your ex
- You ought to let him see the children more

Etc etc ad infinitum.

It's terrible, the way we tell ourselves off. Here we are, in the middle of something horribly painful, and we're still giving ourselves a hard time about it. We can't even get off our own backs. Is this how you'd treat your best friend? Or your child? Or someone you loved?

Scaring Yourself

The inner voice can also be a right drama queen who catastrophizes, as in:

- This is terrible
- I'll never cope alone
- This is all my fault
- This is the worst thing that ever happened and I'll never recover
- You're going to pieces
- I'm going mad

Etc etc ad infinitum.

At least obsession distracts us. The other two mind games do us no good whatsoever. Beating ourselves up creates 'I'm bad' feelings and low self esteem. Scaring ourselves only stirs up worry and panic.

The good news is, you can start to tame this voice down. You can choose not to listen to it. And it *is* a choice. If your inner critic was someone you knew, chances are you'd close the door in her face. You certainly wouldn't choose to spend all your time with her. So get her out of your head.

Awareness Exercise

Just as an exercise, start to notice what you're thinking about. For the moment, don't try to change your thoughts (although obviously you can if you choose – you are in charge of what goes on in your own head, after all).

Ask yourself what these thoughts are distracting yourself from. What's underneath the thoughts?

When you're beating yourself up, just notice what you're saying and think of how you'd talk to yourself if you were your own best friend. Or if you really cared about yourself.

Are they really the truth?

Start to think more positively. If it helps, tell yourself: 'Now I choose to think only good things about myself'.

Eventually you'll get so sick of beating yourself up you'll stop it.

If you must indulge yourself in thoughts of how wonderful he was, also give a little mindspace to how unwonderful.

Toxic Thoughts
How Our Thoughts Intensify Emotion

Thoughts which create fear:
How will I cope?
I'll never have children now
What if I never find anyone again? (In fact any thought beginning What if? is suspect)
I'm too old to be starting again
Thoughts which intensify grief:
He was so lovely
That was a stupid thing to do. I'll never find anyone like him again
Thoughts which contribute to depression:
I'm crap at relationships
I'm crap on my own
I don't know how to choose men

I can't cope with this
Thoughts which create resentment / bitterness:
That bastard. I bet he's…
I gave him the best years of my life
It's all his fault
I should never have fallen for him. I should have known he was a bastard from the outset
Thoughts which create jealousy:
That bitch has what I wanted
I bet he's having a wonderful time and never thinks of me
Thoughts which create guilt:
You shouldn't have done (whatever)
You're a bad person
He'll never recover / you've ruined people's lives
Did I do the right thing? In the right way?

Exercise

Using your feelings journal, write down the toxic thoughts of the day, those avenues of thoughts your mind keeps jogging along again and again. Don't censor them as they come out, just keep writing.

Now read them back. Seeing them in black and white, question them. Don't most of them sound harsh? Or plain ridiculous?

Was he really that wonderful? *Was* he that much of a bastard? Does it *really* matter if he's doing blah blah – is it not more important you have peace of mind?

Dismiss the blatantly stupid ones. Notice the ones that might have a grain of truth. There will probably be a few. Write healthier alternatives. Choose to let go of the ones that don't help.

Peace Of Mind Thoughts:

I'm doing just fine
In fact, I'm doing really well
I'll be fine whatever he does
It doesn't matter what he's doing, I'm focussing on me/I'm who matters here
I'm coping really well
I have been through a horrible experience and I'm doing really well
Nothing matters more to me than my own serenity and peace of mind
I choose to think only thoughts which support me and help me
I choose from now on to be really kind to myself
Yes, it was a great relationship but it's over now and I am moving on

My life is full of wonderful things, even without a man
The kids will be fine whatever happens
I am loveable and I know how to love
I deserve love
I am learning from everything that happens to me right now

(Later on we'll look at the power of thought to create your future. For now we're just dealing with stopping you telling yourself off.)

9 tips for dealing with the bad days:

1 Write it all down in your journal
2 Call a friend and admit you're feeling bad and ask them to listen
3 Sit in a chair and feel the worst for ten minutes
4 Say to yourself: What if it was just OK to be this way. What if this was OK?
5 Write him a letter you never send
6 If it's really bad, take a day off and have a 'duvet day' – just do nothing. Stay in bed, drink endless cups of tea
7 Rent a weepy video and let it all hang out
8 Book a holiday, weekend away – some treat to look forward to
9 Write/speak some affirmations from the 'peace of mind thoughts' list above

It might help to know that there are certain stages everyone goes through around grief/upset/mourning, which we'll cover in the next chapter.

Nurturing Yourself

For the first six months after I left my husband I went a bit wild – I was screwing men I hardly knew, smoking too much, not eating properly. But a blind date taught me an important lesson. We were talking about cooking, and I said I didn't really cook much in the last few years with my husband and I wasn't cooking for myself now and I think that's indicative because cooking's seen as a nurturing thing.

And he said, you can nurture yourself. *And that moment I knew I was going to cry. I realized that because I felt so guilty about what I'd done, I was doing things that made me feel worse. If I went with somebody and it was just a screw, that was fine; but if anyone stroked me and was gentle with me I'd be in absolute floods of tears.*

After that blind date it was a gradual process of being nicer to myself. I noticed even little things like if I had a biscuit I would put it on the table, I wouldn't use a plate. Small things like that as well as big things like believing I had to screw everybody I saw. I realized I was behaving almost like someone who cuts themselves, I was being so self-destructive. It was a really horrible time.

And it took me a long time to not feel guilty and think 'yes someone can be nice to me and that's ok, I'm not such a terrible person'.

Lynsey, 32, on self-neglect

It may be guilt, it may just be habit, but self-neglect is a common response to despair.

And women seem especially prone to it, for two reasons:

- Often we are better at looking after other people than we are at looking after ourselves. This is not surprising, it is how we are brought up. We are conditioned to be caretakers.
- Women, more than men, tend to turn things in on ourselves, blame ourselves when things go wrong. Like Lynsey, above. Even though her heart told her to leave her marriage, her mind wouldn't leave her alone. So she punished herself in various ways.

So a crucial part of building a relationship with yourself while you're single is nurturing yourself – not only bothering to put that biscuit on a plate, but cooking yourself nice meals, giving yourself treats etc. Treating yourself as well as you would a partner or best friend who has been through a traumatic time.

According to research by relationships organization One Plus One, divorcees tend to be less healthy mentally and physically and are four times more likely to commit suicide than married people. And you don't have to have been married to experience the loss of touch and intimacy which affects the immune system as well as the heart.

Gently ask yourself, what do I need? What would make me feel good? It might be to go out and buy yourself a teddy, or a trip to the theatre. Give yourself things you wish a partner would give you. Send yourself flowers on Valentine's Day or your birthday.

It might mean calling a friend every day for support. Or taking an evening class or learning to drive. It might mean a weekly massage or fresh flowers in your bedroom. Whatever means luxury to you – give it to yourself because you deserve it. Get yourself a kitten. Buy Belgian truffles rather than Milk Tray. Have a candlelit dinner with yourself.

Do whatever means taking care of yourself to you. It might mean tidying up. It might mean letting the place get untidy for once.

For me, it was buying myself scented candles. I kept giving them to everyone else, became an expert on which ones smelt best, but I didn't have any in my own home. Lighting candles was something I'd only do when there was a man in my home. I'd never do it alone. Then, when I realized what I was doing, one day I went out and bought the biggest, smelliest scented candle I could find. Now every time I light it I'm indulging myself a little bit. Every time I light it I feel cared for.

Being nice to yourself is self-reinforcing. It reminds you that you matter and the more you do it the more you believe it.

10 treats to give yourself while recovering:

1. Buy some really special bubble bath and *indulge*
2. Remember Café Lonely? Go to a café and have your favourite café mocha with double cream and a chocolate flake
3. Book a facial
4. Or a massage
5. Go buy fluffy, toe-snuggly socks
6. Light some scented candles – just for you
7. Buy champagne, smoked salmon, foie gras
8. Book a holiday or weekend away
9. Yes, go on then, a new outfit (a wonderful indulgence is new underwear when there's only you to see it!)
10. Invest in a cuddly toy – and cuddle it

CHAPTER 5

From Agony to Equilibrium
The seven stages of a successful singleton

Here they are. The varieties of scenery you're likely to see on your journey back to happiness, before you get to park your car in the bay marked 'loving it'.

Remember, this is not a blueprint. There are no hard and fast rules. It's a guide, not a map.

These stages, though typical, last different lengths of time for different people, and different people do them in different orders. And not all seven happen to everyone. If your last relationship wasn't long-term or mightily significant you are likely to avoid plunging into grief. And if by nature you're a very sensible person you may well sidestep stage two and not do anything daft.

Also, you may ping-pong back and forth between stages. You may pass through three, say, and suddenly give going mad a little revisit. When pre-menstrual you may go through all seven in a day!

Either way, it's useful to know that any and all of these stages are part of the natural process called walking back to happiness.

(One last thing to remember – your emotional weather will continue to change day by day, it's just that these ongoing themes are likely.)

Stage 1: Why Me?

Chief characteristics: Shock, disbelief, maybe even denial, despair or numbness.
Duration: A few hours to a few weeks.

At first, you can't quite believe it. You feel numb. You walk around in a trance. You can think of nothing else but you can't think straight anyway. You may burst into fearful, panicky tears a lot, every time the bitter truth hits you.

This stage is always a little mollified if it was you who instigated the break-up, or if it was a long time a-coming, because you were probably mentally preparing yourself. Even so, even if it was *you* who uttered those potent words – 'It's over' – you can have a little reaction along the lines of 'aaargh!, this is really *it*'.

But if he is the breaker and you the unsuspecting breakee, this stage can be profound. And can even last several weeks. Your mind floods with questions – about the future, about the past. But answers are sadly lacking.
A typical experience: Immediately after Selina's boyfriend told her he'd been having an affair and took his stuff and left, she felt she had to 'leave the house and go for a

walk. I was dazed and to this day I haven't the faintest memory where I went. I know I sat on a park bench somewhere while a million questions spun round my head: Where? When? How? *Why*? You start putting the first pieces of the jigsaw in place.'

What you need: Talk, talk and talk some more. This is when your friends will buzz round, so take advantage and talk out every little detail again and again until your frazzled mind begins to get a handle on what happened.

What to avoid: Denial. Some people go into ostrich mode – the this-can't-really-be-happening-so-I'll-just-ignore-it-then syndrome. Denial is a Bad Thing. It keeps you hanging on to a dead relationship, alienates friends and generally prolongs the agony.

Stage 2: Going Mad

Chief characteristics: Drinking too much, sudden outbursts of promiscuity, mad decisions, riding a wild, unpredictable emotional roller-coaster.

Duration: Could be a day, a lost weekend, a few weeks, or several months.

This is where a sudden wild adrenalin-fuelled freedom hits you and you basically go a bit bonkers. Bonkersness manifests in a variety of ways, according to personality. You may sleep with every man you meet, or decide to paint your bedroom walls metallic black, just because you can.

A week after my second husband moved out, I became possessed of a desire to move to Brighton – a town I do not know and where I have no friends. It would have been sheer madness at that moment to abandon my support network just when I needed them most and up sticks to somewhere else, but as I trundled the streets looking at properties the thought seemed entirely plausible. The basic illogical logic went: Most of my life has changed, I might as well change *everything*. Thank God most Brighton houses have small gardens or I'd have sent my stress levels soaring and made a huge move I undoubtedly would have regretted.

A typical experience: Ella, 26, says of breaking up with her six-year relationship: 'At first I went completely off my trolley, doing all the things my boyfriend wouldn't have approved of. I made friends with people who all seemed to have very exciting lives. One of them was very hedonistic and was instrumental in introducing me to going out and getting drunk and not caring what anyone thought, going to amazing parties. It was exhausting, but fun for a while. I felt completely demob happy.'

What you need: Going mad is actually a response to deep pain and despair. You're like pre-war Berlin. You know something horrible is about to hit you, so you might as well make wild, adrenalin-fuelled hay while the sun shines. If you wish for more balance, you could give the

pain and despair a little more room, a little more attention. It will let some of the air out of your pressure cooker.
What to avoid: Doing anything *too* mad. Have a good time, by all means, but don't do anything that could make life any worse or more complicated. So, don't buy that house; don't sleep with that unfeasible man without a condom.

Stage 3: Searching

Chief characteristics: Trying to recreate the lost relationship, either with him, or someone else.
Duration: Anything from days to years!

It's very common, after the shock has worn off and the going mad has lost its novelty, to yearn for what you had. Even if what you had was sub-acceptable. Maybe since the break-up you've had bad experiences, maybe you've got lonely, maybe he's found someone else and you're narked, maybe the children are suffering, whatever. This is when you're vulnerable to a tiny voice in your head which says: Man! Back! US self-help guru Harriet Lerner calls this the 'change back' reaction. Your life has changed dramatically and, after a while, a little impulse sets in which screams 'change back!'. It was comfortable how it was before. It's a scary world out there! Even if you were the one who ended it, you can suddenly find yourself regretting it and pining nostalgically for cosy nights in with a pizza and *him*.

So, you either humiliate yourself before your ex-partner, or you fall hook, line and sinker for someone else and go about trying to mould that someone into the something you had before.

A typical experience: 30-year-old Louise had already fallen out of love with her husband when he announced an affair with a colleague from work and left her. Yet, she says, five months afterwards, she tried hard to get him back. 'The children were missing their dad. They saw him at weekends, but still missed him in the week and, even though it was him who left, I felt so guilty. Plus, I'd been to singles night at the local pub a few times and it was so depressing I thought maybe he wasn't such a rank old sod. So, one night when I knew she was away, I put on some make-up and stockings and went round there, intending to seduce him. I surprised myself by bursting into tears and begging him to come back. He was very kind and sweet and said, Lou, be reasonable, and took me home. I could barely look him in the eye for a couple of weeks after that but I had to do it, I had to give it one final go to know it was truly over.'

What you need: To be brutally honest, hardly anyone gets any joy out of this phase. Ask yourself what you're trying to avoid. Tell friends what's going on and get them to talk you out of it. This is a time when holding still with your emotions and impulses really pays dividends. Call a friend

instead, and if the impulse really doesn't go away after a few days, then you know it's genuine and you can act on it.
What to avoid: 1) Humiliating yourself. 2) Doing something you'll later regret. And 3) *any* action fuelled primarily by alcohol!
(For more on rebound relationships, see Chapter 7.)

Stage 4: Finding Yourself

Chief characteristics: New haircut, new wardrobe, bursting into tears unexpectedly, calming down if you've gone mad.
Duration: Whatever, may come and go as time goes by. The disbelief has worn off, the going mad has lost its novelty and your Man! Back! efforts have proved redundant. Finally it hits you that you really do have to make your life work on your own. You have two emotional tasks to negotiate: mourning the relationship and making a new life for yourself. You're besieged by loss – not just him, but home, family and friends (his) and that comforting sense of being half of a couple. Now you're one whole of a single, but who *are* you?
A typical experience: 26-year-old Elaine's long-term live-in love was a DJ. After the split, she decided to take herself off to HMV to buy ten CDs as a treat. Two minutes flicking through the shelves she burst into tears. 'I couldn't

find 10. I didn't know what kind of music I liked. This really sweet boy serving there said "Are you all right?" and I wailed "I don't know what I like!" It seemed horribly symbolic of how I'd lost sight of who I was.'

What you need: To feel all the feelings and really nurture yourself. (*See page* 55.)

What to avoid: Because this is when painful feelings tend to surface, feel them. Use all the tips on dealing with the feelings in the last chapter.

Stage 5: Men Keep Out!

Chief characteristics: Anger, anger and more anger.

Duration: Usually never longer than a few weeks. (Do not panic – you will not be bitter for the rest of your life.)

One morning you wake up and you think 'All men can bugger off. I'm never falling in love again. I'll get 12 cats, and end up an eccentric old woman in a purple hat, carrying kittens round in a bag.' Or somesuch. Welcome to anger, a vital stage in your healing process.

Of course, it may all focus on your ex. It may be that you want to be carrying him round in a bag, preferably in separate pieces. Which is all fine and dandy too, as long as you don't act on it. Psychologists and bereavement experts agree that anger is a healthy and necessary stage of recovery from grief and loss. When someone dies, their loved ones usually go through a phase of being furious at them for going. How much more appropriate then, when the person concerned has gone off with that tart from accounts.

A typical experience: On New Year's Day, Marion's partner announced he was off to live with another woman, and was gone in 10 minutes. For weeks Marion told friends, 'I bear him no ill-will'. Then, one day, she got a letter from his solicitors claiming half her flat, and she snapped. 'I became about as full of ill-will as it's possible to be. The fact he could be such a shit set me off into complete fury. But it did me good – it shattered all my illusions about him.'

What you need: Anger needs expression like crying needs tears. Allow your anger. Take yourself off for a huffy stomp in the woods. Kick a few trees. Ring your ex and give him what for. Indulge your revenge fantasies. Psychologists say angry fantasies perform a very useful purpose in the psyche. Just don't *act* on them – you don't want to be spending the other stages of singledom at Her Majesty's Pleasure.

What to avoid: Violence, going too far, doing anything you'll regret or will have to account for in a court of law. Also, never, ever turn your anger in on yourself. That leads to disabling depression and low self-esteem as you drive yourself crazy with 'should haves'.

Stage 6: Grief

Chief characteristics: Regrets, guilt, despair, terrible pain and hurt.
Duration: Probably a few weeks at the most, although every hour feels like a lifetime.

Your heart hurts. It *hurts*. Your life seems suddenly pointless. You are going through the motions. Other people appear ridiculously shallow and are living charmed lives as you heave around a throbbing pustule of despair. This phase typically comes on six months after a break-up when other factors like shock and going mad have worked their way through your system and the terrible pain remains. At its mildest form, it's sadness and regret. Some lucky people avoid this phase altogether, and it's more likely after the death of a significant relationship than a brief fling.

What's happening is you are mourning your loss. Another factor that makes grief more likely is when you've suffered other life losses. Or you've had a rebound affair with an unfeasible slob and the realization that that relationship didn't work either plunges you into despair. It can be very tough because your friends think you should be *over it by now*.

Your mind tends to drive you mad with useless regrets: Maybe I didn't take enough care of the relationship. Maybe he wasn't so bad. What if I never find anyone else? All of which is poison to the self-esteem, which needs bolstering, not strychnine.

A typical experience: Rosa says: 'I'd wake up and just not want to get out of bed. I'd hang on in there until the last possible minute, then walk to work feeling like there was a big hole in my chest and everyone could see it. Work would seem pointless. I'd hardly be able to get a tenth of my normal workload done. Then I'd go home at the end of the day and the minute my front door closed behind me I'd cry again. Big wracking sobs in a foetal position. It went on like that for weeks.'

What you need: To remember you have to hit rock bottom to truly recover; that after the darkest hour, comes the dawn etc. You need support – tell friends what you're going through; isolating yourself in your agony will only make it worse.

What to avoid: Running away from this stage by distractions such as a relationship, drugs, sex. It won't work. Grief has a habit of catching up with you.

Stage 7: Single And Loving It!

Chief characteristics: You feel strong, steady and single; you're ready to flirt for England as your sense of attractiveness and joie de vivre returns.

Duration: As long as you wish!

The final achievement of this stage may be preceded by a period of resignation when the pain has deadened but the joie de vivre has yet to make an appearance. Then, one day, you wake up and your first thought on waking isn't a sad, grouchy hmmm, it's a light, thrumming *hmmmm*!

Or maybe feeling better creeps up on you slowly and you realize you haven't thought about your ex for a week, haven't cried for weeks.

Even if you fell in love with someone else on week two, you might still go through all these stages and arrive at a sense of satisfaction with yourself and your new partner when you notice you're suddenly less tense, more available.

A typical experience: Sue discovered on holiday that, at last, she felt better: 'I went on holiday with a girlfriend. I wasn't really looking forward to it that much because I'd been feeling so depressed. But I've never laughed so much in my life, and I discovered by the end of the fortnight, I was hardly thinking about Steve at all. My friend Sara said: You look so much better. And I was. I went back home a different person.'

What you need: To revel in the relief and enjoy yourself.

What to avoid: Getting caught up in another difficult or draining relationship. A life-enhancing, sexually-thrilling relationship is fine, just no difficult or draining ones please.

What if I get stuck?

If you get stuck anywhere and it's gone beyond three months, consider getting help. See your doctor, see a therapist. Do something. You don't have to struggle along with this all by yourself.

Exercise

Write in your journal or talk to a friend about the stages you've been through so far and where you feel you're at.

Wherever you are, congratulate yourself for it!

CHAPTER 6

Sex with your Ex ... and other Ex-Matters

When you are single I think you should stop seeing your ex. It's easier. You're being a fool to yourself and to them, probably, to try to see them. People say let's try and see each other, let's be friends, but if you really want to get on with your life and move things along, once you've sorted all the details out, it's better not to have contact, at least for a while.

Jacqui, speaking from experience

To meet, or not to meet, that is the question. Whether 'tis better to see your ex and moon about the good old days, or whether 'tis better to suffer a good clean break.

All the women I canvassed on this subject believe that it's best to have a break – at least for a while.

When I think of my own experience with exes, there are some I couldn't bear to see afterwards, and a couple who became great friends. Even the one who is now one of my closest male friends, I couldn't see for about six weeks after our break-up. I needed a period of breathing space. A straw poll of the women I spoke to for this book revealed that most managed to become friends with some exes and not others. Every woman had at least one ex they would never want to see again in a million eons.

But, as with anything that involves the human heart, we're all different. It may be that you need to let go gradually. And you may need to see him to do that, or not see him to do that.

What you want to avoid, at all costs, however, is staying attached even though you're no longer in a relationship. Symptoms you're still attached include:

- Thinking/obsessing about him all the time
- Having sex with him
- Talking to him all night at parties
- Calling him to ask his advice all the time. 'He knows more about my finances than anyone else and I trust him'
- He calls you to ask your advice/help all the time. It's the 'No one understands me like you do' syndrome
- Having some financial bond – he's still paying your phone bill or he still owes you money
- Having some area of unfinished business you could clear fairly easily – like all his CDs are still in your flat, or your summer wardrobe is still in his loft
- Wanting to tell him every little detail of your new lovelife (are you trying to make him jealous?)
- Thinking about him while you're having sex with a new partner
- He's still the only male in your life – you don't have any other male friends you talk to

Of course, if you have children the whole thing is hugely complicated. There is one enormous, important area where you will always stay attached; and there is not the possibility of not seeing one another. You will have to, for the sake of the children. It is still possible, however, to let go emotionally even of the father of your child.

And if you're still having sex, believe me, you haven't let go. Sex arouses feelings of attachment – there is a theory that if a woman orgasms with a man it releases an attachment hormone in her system. There's another esoteric theory that men give women their energy when they have sex, and it hangs around. Either way, sex also creates and maintains an emotional bond. You're setting yourself up to be hurt some more and, at best, prolonging the agony. Don't go back in that muddy puddle. Get out of it and wipe down your wellingtons. You will feel better for it, honestly.

'I had this disastrous relationship with a gorgeous man. And although we just couldn't seem to get on, the sex was amazing. Maybe because we couldn't get on, the sex was amazing. Anyway, after we split up, we met up and tried to be friends, but we always ended up in bed. I just couldn't help myself, my body would go mad when he was around. But every single time, after my lust was slaked, as it were, I thought, oh no. And I'd feel I'd got myself all entangled with him again. And he'd start calling me and the whole mad shouting match would begin all over. Finally, one day, I called him up and said I am never going to have sex with you

again. He was furious, but the relief I felt made it all worth while. And only then did I start to get over him.'

Rosa

Of course an ex can turn into a valuable friend, but you owe it to yourself to make sure that's all he is and not a crutch you lean on in order to avoid taking responsibility for your own life.

Letting Go Of Your Ex

If you feel you are still attached, there are things you can do to let go:

It's good to talk

Number one is communicate. Tell him 'This isn't working for me, seeing you so often'.

Or…

'This isn't working for me, still having sex with you. It prevents me letting go and moving on and although I'm fond of you I'm not going to do it anymore. Please help me with this by leaving me alone.'

Or…

'I feel I'm seeing you too often and what I realize is once a month would work better for me.'

or whatever.

These are just examples. The main thing to remember is you're not responsible for his life and his feelings. And you have the right to lead your life the way you want to. Even if you ended it and he's hurt, you're not beholden to him.

Invoking Ritual

Somewhere in the Dickensian sludge under the Thames by Blackfriar's Bridge lies my wedding ring. It was also my grandmother's wedding ring – I had it made smaller to fit me for my first marriage. And throwing it away felt hugely liberating.

I flung it over the bridge on the night of a new moon shortly before I married for a second time. It was my way of saying goodbye to the old before taking on the new.

I'd already done several things to let go of my first husband – making the decision not to have any contact with him, clearing out all his photographs, had a 'divorce party' for my girlfriends, but I felt I needed a little more. One more conscious ending.

This need not be as silly as it sounds. We have an abundance of ritual around marriage in our society, but nothing around divorce. Couples never get the chance to look one another in the eye and pronounce 'I don't' the way they whisper 'I do'. Yet, just as a funeral becomes the focus and catharsis for grief after a death, it is useful to have some little letting go ritual to mark a break-up.

(In America there's a place where divorcees can take their wedding rings and beat the hell out of them on a forge to create some other gold object. It's a cathartic, transformational experience, apparently.)

If you didn't tie the knot, there is nothing at all to mark the passing of what may have been a deeply significant chunk of your life. You may have lived together for seven years, yet when you split, your Granny says: 'Well, it wasn't as if you were married.' So it's up to you create some little conscious act that acknowledges 'That's that, then'.

Some suggestions:

- Have a girls-only party. Invite your posse of supportive friends round, get the champagne in and celebrate. Rosa says: 'I had an evening with about seven girlfriends and the highlight was burning a picture of me and him together. We all shrieked our heads off as he disappeared up the chimney.'
- A powerful private ritual is to write a letter to him where you list all your resentments and regrets about him, then burn it. Or just list your feelings about the relationship – then burn that. Watch your old relationship go up in smoke.
- Go the whole emotional hog and make a pilgrimage to some place that meant a lot to the pair of you and say goodbye there. Leah says: 'I drove to Hastings,

which is where we went for our first weekend away together. On the way down I played music that reminded me of him – as I cried my eyes out – and when I got to the sea I threw in all our photographs, letters he'd written me, everything. Then I felt hugely better and went and had a cream tea all by myself. I did feel lighter afterwards.'

- It is incredibly powerful to do some ritual with your ex, even if it's only a conversation where you actually talk, tell one another what you loved and what you miss. So many relationships end in pain and confusion. When you have an 'ending' conversation, especially where you really listen to one another, it helps you move on. Ella says: 'We met up and took it in turns to clarify why exactly we were breaking up, how we felt about it, the great times we remembered and what we'd miss. I honestly think if we hadn't done that we wouldn't be the great friends we are today.'

A Word On Friends

Oh, him. He had big ears anyway.

Rosa's best friend's inevitable pronouncement whenever she splits up with anyone

When my first marriage ended I was the 'innocent victim' of an affair I knew nothing about. Friends rallied round. The day it happened, my friend Ginny came and picked me up and let me live in her house for six months – an amazing act of generosity way above and beyond the call of best-friend duty.

I was blessed with huge doses of sympathy and unconditional support. Plus my husband broke contact with virtually all our friends, so it was relatively easy on that front too.

When I split up from my second marriage it was a whole different ball game. And much, much more complicated. I found my friendships shift and change like quicksand. And that was scary. My friends are my bedrock.

It was tricky because this time I was the one who ended it and after only a year.

Firstly I realized this challenged people's hopes for us. They'd bought into the wonderful dream we'd spun at our wedding and couldn't bear to see it dashed so soon. Because they loved us, they wanted it to work. And because they hadn't lived with our difficulties day by day, they couldn't quite believe it hadn't worked. *Are you sure? How could you? Give it time*. Everyone had a stance, a theory, a suggestion. I was deluged with advice and questions at a time when it was difficult enough working out my own convictions and sticking to them.

Which is all fair enough. It's what friends do.

Then there was my ex. Unlike ex no.1, ex no.2 wanted to make elaborate, ceremonial farewells to all my closest friends. Again fair enough, some had become his friends, some continue to be his friends. And as one of them pointed out: 'Eighteen months ago you were wanting us all to love him. You can't just expect us all to drop him now just because you have.'

But you can't help that indignant, whiny: 'But he/she was my friend first!' as though friends can be sifted as easily as the CD collection.

Plus, a part of me felt guilty so I was incredibly sensitive to criticism. I expected some people to judge me, and they did. Unreasonably – but who said breaking up is ever reasonable? – I wanted everyone to approve of me, love me, understand me and some of them just didn't. Even if they loved me, they didn't approve or understand. I had to learn to live with this disapproval and other people's confusion.

I found myself up against stiff decisions like: Do I still love this person even though I'm cross with her because of what she said last Wednesday? And the answer was usually yes. I learnt, to come over all new-agey for a moment, about forgiveness and unconditional love.

All this forgiving and life going on and getting over it felt very grown up. Sometimes it was more painful than the break-up – I had more practice and experience at that. But falling out with friends hadn't happened since school. It was all very bewildering.

I learnt how, ultimately, I'm the only person whose opinions matter because – as George Michael puts it in his song 'Jesus To A Child' – 'I'm the only one/Living in my life'. I learnt you can't please all of the people all of the time. And that being disapproved of by your closest friends and family is a sobering and painful experience. Words like responsibility and consequences took on another layer of meaning. They became experiences, not just words.

I even had trouble with my best friend, which wobbled me no end. She couldn't stand my neediness and her ability to call a spade not just a spade but a blunt instrument with shit on it was an issue once or twice. I felt alone and helpless. It was like I'd thrown all my relationships up in the air and had no idea where they would all settle.

Some people I felt embarrassed to contact. Some I hadn't seen since our wedding to suddenly tell them now it's all over. And I felt like I could only handle so much at a time.

The good news, to coin a cliché, is I really found out who my friends are. The ones who understood, or who stuck with me even if they didn't understand, were like gold dust. And there were lots of them. I actually have better relationships with some, based on truth. We've been through the worst together and come through. As my best friend put it: surely honesty is better and more real in a friendship than pretending. And when you know people disapprove of your behaviour but still love you, that's very enriching.

At the end of the day, when your ability and confidence in yourself around relationships is at a low ebb anyway, it's good – very good – to know you've got friends.

Points to remember when dealing with friends:

- Try not to take it all too personally. Any action has consequences and sometimes they are unpleasant.
- Remember, you are very vulnerable right now and you don't have to put up with any crap.
- Remember a break-up unsettles people. It puts doubts into their heads about their own relationships. It reminds them their own affairs could go belly-up at any time. They look at you and think 'There but for the grace of God go I…' And that's scary and discomforts people.
- Or, maybe some of your friends are stuck in a terrible relationship and your sudden singleness brings up barely-conscious feelings of envy which they subtly take out on you. These are the ones who don't want to hear you're doing well; don't want to hear what fun you had on your one-night stand last Thursday. With these people you just have to realize 'This is their stuff', stand up for yourself and leave them alone.
- Some people just can't cope with the intensity of your feelings – your grief, your anger. It reminds them of painful past experiences they'd rather not remember or unresolved feelings they're sitting on and would rather not think about. These people are the ones who

act uncomfortable, or who tell you to pull yourself together.

- And some just aren't very sympathetic. They get bored with your ongoing getting-over-it drama, leaving you feeling like a neurotic wreck.
- Worst of all are the ones who feel threatened. Fearing that you might run off with their husband. Or who can only cope with other couples. You may find – although this is more common for men – that you don't have any friends who are single and your coupley friends suddenly cool off.

Exercise

Consciously create a support network. Make a list of the friends who sympathize and support you. Make a list of the ones who don't. Know who supports you and who doesn't. Don't waste time and effort trying to pursuade the ones who don't. Protect yourself, don't be around negative people who make you doubt yourself.

Ask for help. Ask for a 15 minute moan. Then shut up and listen to them. Don't get self-absorbed. It won't do you any good and will alienate your friends if you're all take and no give.

Tell safe people what you need and how you are. They're the people you call and say 'This is how I feel today'. Toxic ones are the ones you stop calling.

Maybe there are some people you'd like to spend more time with. This is an ideal time to make new friends. If there's anyone you want to spend less time with, do it. If you need new friends, ask people.

Points to remember:

- You don't have to keep justifying yourself. The only person whose approval and opinion truly matters is yourself. The others aren't living in your life.
- You don't have to see people you don't like. You have the right to spend your precious time as you see fit, with people who love and nurture you and have your welfare at heart.
- Now is a good time to practise being selfish. Say, I really need a lot of time alone right now and I'm not going out much or fixing up much. They'll probably get the message. If not, you will have to be more assertive about it.

The delights of the barrier bonk!

'After six or eight weeks of being single my friend Pete said what you need is a bonk. I said I have no idea how to do a one-night stand. He said, don't worry, leave it up to me. He was having this party for his best friend and he told me, don't bring anyone except maybe a single girlfriend. I got to the restaurant and I swear there were 26 men around the table. None of them, if they had girlfriends, had been allowed to bring them. One

vodka and tonic later Pete sidled up to me and said: You just tell me which one you like and I'll make sure it happens. All these men are here to serve you. You're an attractive woman, any one of them would be happy to have you.

I picked one I'd met before and Pete said to him: Take her home in a minicab and be good to her. Because we were both drunk, it was probably the worst sex of my entire life, but worth it. He kindly spread the word I was fantastic in bed, which boosted my ego in a way that needed to be boosted. During the last two years of my relationship we hadn't had sex and I'd completely lost my confidence. The barrier bonk definitely put it back!'

Ella, 26, on getting back in the saddle

As tactics go, it can be more fun than any amount of howling at the moon. The barrier bonk is so called because it puts a barrier between you and the memory of your ex. Even if, as with Ella, above, the sex isn't that great, the barrier bonk can make you feel desirable again.

Often in the long decline of a relationship your sexual self-image takes a battering. Maybe you've been rejected and you doubt your attractiveness; maybe the passion went out of the relationship and you're horribly out of practice. As another barrier bonker confesses...

When I split up with John I was missing sex greatly and I had real insecurities about my body because he was always criticizing it – saying I was too fat and so on. Someone said to me there's always a Mr or Mrs Interim, and once you've had sex with someone else you have a completely different view on your old relationship. So I made a conscious decision to go and see my ex-husband – the man I'd had the best sex of my life with. I knew if he was single I'd contrive to sleep with him again. It was his birthday and I sent him 25 sunflowers. I knew that would do two things: one, it would please him, and two, he'd phone me. And he did.

We went out for a drink and made love all night. And it was good for me in several ways: because sex hadn't been good with John, and it was fabulous with my ex-husband, it reminded me how good sex is important in my life; it proved to me I could be sexy and desirable again, after the battering my self-image had taken with John; and it acted as a great 'fuck you', which was significant in the power game I was in with John at the time. After that weekend I knew he knew somehow I was different. He didn't know why, but I did! It was as if I'd written 'I'm shagging someone' across my forehead in a neon light only he could see.

Therese, 28

The downside of the barrier bonk is that bonking – any bonking – can get complicated. You might get hurt again. You might hurt someone else again. You have to weigh up the risks, take a deep breath and start again.

Some tips:

- Try not to fall in love with them, especially if they're clear there are no strings.
- Don't go with anyone who's going to hurt you.
- Don't do anything daft – remember: **condoms**.

CHAPTER 7

The Ups and Downs of the Rebound Relationship

Just as I was splitting up with Robin I met this man who, looking back on it, was everything Robin was not. He was fun where Robin was serious; he was big where Robin was quite wiry; he was spontaneous where Robin was very controlled. And we plunged into a wild, whirlwind affair. Sex was amazing, and we laughed until we got bellyache. I fell crashingly in love and, I realize now, got very intense very quickly, and it scared him off. If only I'd taken things a little more slowly. But I think I was desperately trying to recreate another relationship to persuade myself I was OK. And, when you're on the rebound, you do some very strange things...

Therese, on love on the bounce

The chief characteristic of the rebound relationship is the lover you find will be exactly the opposite of the lover you just lost. If your last relationship broke up because your ex was treating you so much like part of the furniture that he was stacking his magazines under your arm, Mr Rebound will be so attentive you'll be prising him off with a vice. If your last one smothered so much you could hardly breathe – voila! – you will manifest a mean, moody, cold personage who'll so give you the runaround you'll feel like the M25.

The other main characteristic is he arrives at a time when you know you're not really ready. But, hell, you do it anyway.

Rebound affairs usually blossom between three and six months after The Biggie – at that vulnerable point when the relief of the big escape has faded and the No. 1 Panic – *'What if I never find anyone ever again?'* – is beginning to kick in. But, the truth is, you're not ready and your judgement is likely to be – at best – iffy.

Consequently, rebound affairs tend to be at their mildest unsatisfactory and at worst layer trauma upon more trauma like a nightmare lasagne. But knowing that doesn't stop us.

My second husband was a nice Jewish boy. There was nothing nice about Mr Next. He didn't look nice, he looked trouble. He didn't have a job and he didn't seem to like me doing mine. He was evasive, ambiguous and everything my mother would have disapproved of when I was 15. A throwback to an earlier form of rebellion.

AND I DID IT ANYWAY.

One of my friends, in a moment of literary inspiration, quoted William Blake at me. Something about it is better to murder a babe in its cradle than nurse an unfulfilled desire. Which seemed a bit harsh. Yet not inappropriate. I felt propelled by an ancient pattern. *I must have a man in my life or else. I must have a man in my life or else.* By the end of the relationship, a few months down the line, I realized it had turned into 'I must have a man or else I might get happy and healthy and find out about myself and how scary would that be?' At length I decided: not too scary to give it a go.

The relationship wasn't good for me – it was draining and exhausting; I wasn't available to him and no doubt added to his personal pain stores. And I don't regret it a bit. I learnt a lot from it. I learnt that you learn from everything. I learnt that I *really* wasn't ready for another relationship and wasn't willing to go on conning myself – and hurting other people in the process. I learnt I wasn't prepared to put up with any old difficulty just to have someone in my life. I learnt I deserve more than crumbs from a cold man's table and I really believe that now.

Yet there were wonderful payoffs. Romantic, neon-lit walks in London at sunset when I saw the city I live in literally in a different light. Eating chocolate ice-cream in bed, getting it all over the sheets and not giving a monkey's. Days spent in bed together talking, making love and getting up only for aforementioned sunset walks. Cosy evenings on the sofa together watching *Who Wants to Be a Millionaire* and shrieking the answers at the screen. And amazing, amazing sex. (What is the point of a rebound relationship if you're not having amazing sex?) It was an important time and – to coin a cliché – a little part of me will always love him.

But there were abundant difficulties – including my own erratic behaviour which I mainly put down to the fact

I could have been the character in the film *This Year's Love* who leaps into bed with a man and says: I'm on the rebound and I'm not to be trusted. So, I said hello to that spectre at the sex-feast of the rebound affair: guilt. If Mr Rebound has any feelings for you at all – and sod's law says he will – you will end up feeling awful for behaving like a heel. Or, as one of my girlfriends put it, like a man.

And when it was all over, at least I had gained a new kind of confidence from the thought: if that's the best I can manage right now, then I'd better get on with managing nothing.

So. If you find yourself in or about to embark on a rebound relationship, you could speed the whole process by asking yourself these questions:

When I weigh up the payoffs against the difficulties, is it worth it?

Is he so the antithesis of my ex that I'm just acting out a form of rebellion?

Am I actually having a good time here?

Am I in my right mind?

Summary of part one

In order to achieve an ending on your last relationship, you are…

- Quitting blaming him for everything that's wrong in your life
- Building on your self-awareness
- Feeling your feelings – not distracting yourself from them
- Thinking in positive ways that support you
- Consciously nurturing yourself
- Gaining an awareness of the stages of single and know where you are
- Separating yourself from your ex so as to achieve a clean break
- Building a group of supportive friends
- Maybe having a barrier bonk or rebound relationship!

PART 2

A Love Affair with Yourself

Now is the time to focus on the one person who really matters: ***you.***

Note: if you're dating, in a rebound relationship or have fallen suddenly, stonkingly in love, you can still benefit enormously from reading and working with this part.

10 women explain how being single builds your self-esteem

My first relationship broke up when I left university and he just stopped coming round. My reaction to that was to go into a massive depression. I was in a cynical state of mind and very self-destructive. I started having one-night-stands and I chose awful men, but at least I could console myself with the fact that if this is what all men are like then it's good my first love left me. It was horrible, and I made myself worse. It got to the lowest point when I had a relationship with someone who was the pinnacle of all these bad relationships, then I found out he was having a relationship with his ex-girlfriend all the time he was with me. I really hit rock bottom. I was put on Prozac at that point. That was how bad it got before I realized that being single was better.

If I think of it as a graph where the bottom point is misery and the top is happiness, that was how my relationship with singledom went. Through doing things for myself and living on my own, I learned to like my own self and company. It took me to the bloody age of 25, but I got there.

Ariana, 29

I remember when I was with my ex I always felt I needed someone else to advise me, support me, even pay for me.

I couldn't imagine being totally self-sufficient and I needed someone else to help me survive, even financially. I felt I needed to be dependent on a man, even while knowing that thinking that way is so dodgy, I don't want to feel like this.

It's so different now. I don't feel like that at all any more. I feel completely self-sufficient. Which is not to say I don't want a man, but when one comes along it will be that much more level a relationship because I know I don't *need* him.

Jacqui

I did grow as a person when I was single. I was working on a newspaper and a new editor came who took a real dislike to me and she made me redundant. I had no one to really fall back on but myself. I've never been more determined to survive. And I was so successful. By the end of my notice they were asking me to stay an extra month – and I didn't! I got myself on my own feet. I had no one to nurse me through it so I had to nurse myself and that gave me a real sense of satisfaction. I was very proud of myself. I became happier and more confident as a person, so it was no surprise really when I met someone who was really nice. I was probably in the best possible frame of mind to meet him.

Rachel

After splitting up with my ex I began to feel better about myself than I had for years. I lost a lot of weight, which was almost like emotional weight I'd been carrying. People said I looked really different, and I thought – I can reinvent myself! And that was really exciting. It's no longer always Elaine and Robert but Elaine and Elaine. That made me feel really sexy.

Elaine

It's hard to put into words, but I feel I have more substance.

Sarah

I remember when I went to Israel to work on a kibbutz years ago I thought no one knows me here, I have no partner here, no friends. If they like me it's just because they like me as I stand. Being single is a bit like that. I can be big and loud and noisy. When you have a partner you know they'll support you in that. Now when I'm big and loud and noisy, it just has to be all right for me. In that respect I feel more like I'm living my own life, I'm not leaning into anyone else's approval or disapproval.

Ria

I feel like my heart's more open, and in a less focussed way. In a relationship your heart is often open to just one person, whereas I feel more available to be loving with all sorts of people – like in my work with over-60s. Before, when I got loving feelings for others I thought, oh I feel like this because I'm in love. And something about that makes me feel more me somehow.

Louise

Being single has given me a different view of myself, how I behave and how I work. It's given me a chance to see how valuable I am. Before, I always went after the unobtainable. Now I want someone who will value me and make me feel valued.

Sarah

My observation is I've learned more about myself since I've been single, especially around my neediness and how that makes me intense with men. I think what I'm learning is to be lighter. But there is lots about being single that I really relish, the lack of compromise in my life. There is a part of me that has never explored lots of different areas of myself, my life and what life has to offer me. I never felt in a relationship I could do any of that but I now feel I can. What I have learned is everybody's time for being single is very individual and unique and there is no such thing as a set time to be on your own. I also think that some people will never be on their own. But I wouldn't give up my single status readily. I think I would negotiate a relationship very differently now I've been on my own. There are things I would want to maintain for myself, like nights out with single friends and time for myself to be on my own. I also think I'm clearer about what I'm looking for. It isn't just a man. Someone who will value me, I want to be valued. That's what a relationship for me is all about, that may not be the same for other people.

Therese

I do feel messianic about it. Being single gets such a bad press. I think that's terribly calculated by men, it is obviously in their interests if all women are desperate. A woman who's desperate is going to be much more willing to wash their socks than a woman who isn't. While I was single I had a terrific time and I knew how to be completely independent so that all that traditional man/woman stuff sickens me now. Someone was talking to me the other day about making tea for a cricket match, I wanted to spit! I thought, why are you making tea for a sweaty man on a Saturday afternoon? Bugger me if a man ever cooked a cake for a woman's sewing circle.

Maria

CHAPTER 8

One-der-ful

When people split up, they often say they miss stability and security and that feeling of knowing where they're going, but I actually feel more secure being single. I know where I'm going because it's in my control. That feeling comes when you relax into your single life enough and become confident enough. It's taken me a year of being truly single to reach that place, but now I'm there it's wonderful.

I feel confident I can run my own life and for it to be a great one – far more so than when I was first single. When a man comes into your life it actually brings more uncertainty. But you have to have the confidence that you can give yourself security and you don't need someone else to give it to you. When you can give yourself that, it makes you feel good and strong. Now I know that whatever happens to me, yes, I might be laid low by some things, but I'm always going to survive. I have that feeling inside me and I like having that feeling inside. And I don't think it's a barrier or has made me hard. You only get strength by experiencing things and coming through them.

Jacqui, four years single (on and off)
'since the real biggie'

So. You're single. Congratulations. Whether your state is temporary or permanent, there has never been a better time to be flying solo. As we know from Chapter 1, it's easier and more blissful to be single now than ever before, women have more financial freedom than ever before; single women have more fun than ever before.

Now you can put all your energy and effort into the one relationship that really matters in your life: the one you have with yourself.

The results may amaze you.

The wonderful, relieving fact of singlehood is you never have to do anything you don't want to do. You can say no to the couply brunch, stay in bed all day and eat biscuits. You don't have to be polite to people you don't like because they're *his friends*. You don't have to sit through an evening chowing about football – *unless, of course, you love football*.

Your life, your time, is completely your own. It may feel strange at first, but it's a wonderful freedom. And freedom allows new possibilities to come into your life: new people, new places, new activities.

After a while those pain clouds begin to clear and you have time and energy to realize:

Here I am, me, I'm single. I can do anything I want.

Which begs the question:

So what DO I want?

How Relationships Distract Us From Ourselves

Relationships are riddled with compromise. From the minute you wake up in the morning you're half thinking about him – is he out of the bathroom yet? Is he still in a bad mood? What did he mean by that strange remark last night? All that focus on someone else takes energy.

The degree to which we focus on our partner varies from person to person. Some do it excessively. Like Leah, who says:

At university, even though I was doing just as much work as him, from the moment I started going out with Steve, I used to iron his pants and vests and get up at two in the morning to make rhubarb crumble so he could have it when he came home from the pub because it was his favourite thing in the world. Every morning I'd get up early and take off last night's makeup and put on today's make up so when he woke up I'd be like Doris bloody Day there twinkling at him.

Others of us take a more Jo Brand approach in the adapting ourselves stakes. He gets us without makeup and we don't give a damn. Nonetheless, living with other people, being with other people, naturally distracts us from our relationship with ourselves. Because relating takes up time and energy, you can become so involved in your other half and what they want, or what the pair of you as a couple want, you lose track of you and what *you* want. And need. You're caught up in the drama of trying to figure him out – what he's done *now*, what he's said, what would make him happy, and does he really like you anyway? So much so that you're not figuring out if you like *him*. Or whether constantly trying to figure someone out is what you want and *need* for yourself.

When Isabel was in love with Charlie she moved up to Scotland to be with him. Six months later he left. She says:

I spent a whole day crying, then I thought OK, I need to look at where I am with me, where I am with life. What I realized was my job, which I'd taken in order to relocate and be with him, was not what I really wanted. Also, living in the middle of the Highlands was not what I wanted as a single woman. I thought about what I did want to do and realized I'd always fancied living in London. So why not? I started applying for jobs in the capital and when I got one I felt like a little kid in a brand new toybox. I loved finding out about the city all on my own. I'd take myself off like a tourist at weekends. I just loved *it. And I discovered an independence I never knew I possessed.*

Whoever was responsible for concocting fairy tales like Cinderella and Sleeping Beauty has a lot to answer for. Even though we're sexy, sussed women in a new millenium, we have an unfortunate, archaic tendency to put our lives on hold – when a man comes along it'll all be all right and we'll live happily ever after. Fairy-story thinking not only keeps us stuck and dependent, the responsibility on the poor old dream man is awesome. Your expectations of this white knight in shining armour will be more charged than your favourite credit card. Turn the tables for a minute. Are you looking for a man who is waiting for a woman to make *his* life all right? I don't think so. You need your life to be all right anyway. Right here, right now.

Now there's no one to distract you – at least, not much! – you can get on with figuring yourself out. A far more fascinating and rewarding activity. And a wonderful payoff is when you know yourself, like yourself and trust yourself, like magic you need to spend less time and energy focussed on other people. Somehow it doesn't matter so much. You realize you value yourself too much to be constantly worrying about what's going through his mind.

Who are *you*? Without a partner. Without the role of girlfriend, wife, 'other half'. Now you're half of nothing, you're one whole of a whole. But what shape is that whole? What colour is it? What does it like to do? What tune does it like to dance to?

You can't have an effective, fulfilling relationship with anyone unless you have one with yourself. And now is your chance to discover yourself. Your chance to become entranced by the one person who really matters. To make a commitment to the one person likely to truly repay that commitment in lifelong gratitude.

You.

US relationships expert Dr Stan Charnofsky, in his book *When Women Leave Men,* quotes the famous psychologist Erik Erikson who said there were certain psychological tasks we have to achieve in each stage of life. As teenagers, the task we need to complete is 'identity' – learning to throw off the dictates of parents, teachers, friends and find out who we are. After that, we can negotiate the very adult task of 'intimacy'. We must learn how to negotiate an intimate relationship, or face a lifetime of isolation. For Erikson, the sequence was always identity before intimacy – for how can you learn to have an intimate relationship if you don't know who you are? Charnofsky says: 'I believe that this same sequence and equation occurs at *any time in life when there is a major crisis*. When there is a death, a loss of a job, the end of a relationship, you must find out who you are all over again in the new life situation. The equation holds: identity before intimacy.'

So even if you've been single before and you're thinking, I *did* all this last time, now is the time to rediscover yourself, your new single self. It won't be the same as your old former single self. You will have changed and grown.

This has certainly been true for me. When my second marriage broke down, with its set of wishes, hopes and dreams attendant upon being with that person for the rest of my life and hopefully becoming a parent, I had to ponder: How do I want my life to be if I spend it alone? And if I don't have children? How do I want it to be now? Part of the answer was that I desperately needed a new career challenge. I had been treading water at work for a while, but I wasn't bothered because working from home as a freelance journalist would segue well with motherhood. With that dream out of the window I needed something else – my career re-emerged as important again. Plus, I realized my creativity needed other outlets – I would have to find other ways of making children a part of my life. All this meant I had to take a long, interested look at who I am now, what I want now, where I'm going now.

(The postscript to this story: The one thing I've always wanted to do is write a book. Interestingly, the minute I became single I was having lunch with Mandi Norwood, Cosmo's editor, we talked about it and here it is. Magically, the opportunity I needed appeared. You're reading the fruit of my decision to dream about what I wanted next and have the courage to ask for it.)

You don't want a partner who's never been single. I respect a man who says I'm going off by myself with X. You don't want someone who can't stand their own company.

Maria

It's common that when we're not in a relationship we focus more on our career. But it doesn't have to be all about work. Now you don't have a constant playmate, you can ponder over what games you might like to play on your own.

Now is the ideal time to do all those things you promised yourself 'if only I had the time'. As in: 'If only I had the time I'd go to night school and learn pottery'. 'If only I had the time I'd take piano lessons'. 'Or explore India'. 'Or learn the trapeze'. Now joint wishes, hopes and dreams have died, now is the time to think, what are my wishes, hopes and dreams for myself? What would I like to do today? Tonight? For the rest of my life?

It's time to take your life into your own hands so when a man comes along he'll be a wonderful addition, not a reason for living.

When Leah became single, she decided to fulfill a life-long dream of going to art college. It transformed her life. She says:

It's made me more real. I know who I am and who I'm meant to be and I'm no longer constantly looking for that. I always wanted to go to art college and doing it was so self-affirming. When I got there I felt like I was the person I'd always been meant to be, and, I suppose it took the focus off thinking if I was with a man it would make me the person I'd always been meant to be. On my first day there I was so excited. Actually I felt really sexy, and I understood that sexual excitement is about feeling good about yourself, and it doesn't have to be a man that makes you so. I remember my flat-mate saying to me that while it's obvious I really love my boyfriend now, it amazed him I manage to be my own person and have my own life. As I said, I didn't used to be like that, it's art that's made the difference. People say that when you have children it changes the way you think about relationships because now there's something that's equally important to you. I feel like that about art. And I don't know if I could have got into art so easily if I'd been in a relationship. I rediscovered it as a passion because I was not in a relationship.

Just Do It!

What is it you want to rediscover now you're free as a bird? Be proactive! Do it now! Go to salsa classes. Learn to swim properly. Get a visa and work abroad. Learn French. Change career. Become a therapist. Whatever. As the philosopher Goethe said: 'Whatever you think you can do or believe you can do, begin it. Action has magic, grace and power in it.'

Exercise

Start dreaming

You need to have a dream. 'A goal is only a dream taken seriously,' said a writer called Esther Roberton. Get out your feelings journal and jot down all your wishes, hopes and dreams for yourself. Don't censor what you write, just let it all flow.

Often a big change like becoming single opens the flood-gates for other types of change. Maybe now you can have the career you always wanted without your husband telling you it's mad, or you'll never pay the mortgage. In your extra spare time you can start training for something you've always wanted to do – like writing or becoming a therapist.

Focus on the future

Light a candle and allow yourself to dream.

Think about what you loved to do as a child, the dreams you had for yourself then. Let your mind wander. And forget fear. Maybe you didn't do those things because you were just an eensy bit scared. Just imagine, for the moment, you're as fearless as Arnold Schwarzenegger with something heavy in his hand.

What I would secretly love to do is...

List at least five things

____

____

____

____

____

____

____

____

____

Now you've had fun dreaming, look at your list realistically. Is it really so impossible to do those things? Just pick one thing and do something this week towards making that a possibility. Once you start investigating you get a wonderful buzz that comes with 'This is something I'm doing purely for me, just because I want to.'

Fear and excitement are sometimes the same thing.

Who am I?

This is an exercise in boasting. Just for the sheer pleasurable hell of it.

What are my strengths?
What are my weaknesses?
What do I really love about myself?
What would I like to change about myself?
What do I get complimented on?
What would I love to get complimented on?
What is my vision for my life? What would I like to happen over the next five years?

Make yourself matter

Everyone is special to themselves somewhere. If you think about it, you wouldn't try so hard to succeed at work, or in love, if you didn't believe somewhere you're special. Why is it that with women we have this idea that treating ourselves is bad? Why is doing something that is completely for yourself, like eating in a bloody restaurant, such a huge thing to do? It's not a huge thing to do when you're with someone, when you have someone to back you up. But it can be when you do it purely for yourself. I bet less women go to restaurants on their own than masturbate.

Ariana, 29, single five years

Exercise

Take yourself on a romantic date. Have a bubble bath, put on fresh underwear and make-up, just as though you were going out with a man, but go alone. Go to a fancy restaurant, take a walk in the woods. And talk to yourself as would a lover: 'You look lovely', 'I'm having a wonderful time', 'You're so interesting' and so on. If you want to go the whole hog, you could end the evening making love to yourself and telling yourself afterwards you were hotter in the sack than Sharon Stone on a good day!

Whatever, have fun with it, take some emotional risks, feel silly, nervous, vulnerable. And have a nice time.

Other Tricks To Boost Your Single Self

The point of all these actions is putting energy into your single self.

- Make a shrine to your single self. Set up a small table, a windowsill, or a shelf in your room or flat and fill it with your favourite objects, or things that are meaningful to you in your single life. Like: a wonderful photo of you looking happy and confident; photos of friends who help you; some fresh flowers, favourite images, quotes, knick-knacks; stones, leaves – whatever takes your fancy.
- Go through a bunch of magazines, ripping out images/words/quotes you like. Then make a collage by sticking them on a piece of newspaper. Frame this, or pin it on your wall to remind you how you wish to feel and what you wish to happen in your single life.
- Make a cosmic shopping list! Write out your wishes, hopes and dreams from the exercise earlier and put it in a special vase, hide it behind a favourite picture frame, pin it on the wall. And watch them all come true! Geri Halliwell did this before she was a Spice Girl – and her wishes all came true, apart from marrying George Michael – a sexual impossibility – but even so, she got to be his friend.
- Ask your friends what they like about you and write down all compliments you get in your journal.
- Now is the time to read how you felt when you began the journal and see how, already, you've changed and moved forward.

Self-worth comes from self-work!

21 things you could do now you're single

1. Decorate your flat
2. Buy a flat
3. Travel round the world
4. Take that evening class
5. Learn a language
6. Do yoga/meditate
7. Join that gym you've been walking past each morning
8. Teach yourself to cook one dish really well
9. Learn how to use a power drill
10. Fulfill a long-held dream
11. Take a degree via the Open University
12. Change career
13. Get a pet
14. Change your image – get a hair cut, or go blonde
15. Throw out all your old clothes and get a new look
16. Go clubbing again
17. Get therapy
18. Take up a hobby
19. Read *War and Peace*, or *Remembrance of Times Past*, or *A Suitable Boy*, or plough your way through the classics
20. Go on holiday with a girlfriend
21. Move to the city, move to the country, move to another country!

CHAPTER 9

Making the Most of it

Being single is hard work. People say you have to work at a relationship, you have to work at a relationship with yourself too. People say you can take a man for granted. You can take yourself for granted too. If you treat time with yourself as time with someone who's interesting and nice, that's fine; but if you treat time with yourself as time that is by definition not with anyone, you'll be a nobody in your own head.

Maria, campaigner for the single self

Yes, being single is hard work. It can also be exciting, exhilarating, and fun. Especially if you make the most of it and use the time while you're single to do things you'd never dare do, or just plain couldn't do, hunkered down in cosy coupledom.

The more you take advantage of single pleasures, from a night in alone to travelling round the world by yourself, the more you become reconciled to your single state. Instead as a gap between the things in life which are truly worthwhile, you will begin to realize that single is fun, you may also have some of the most amazing moments of your life.

You also learn a lot about you, you develop independence, self-sufficiency. And you gain enormous confidence from knowing you can cope with whatever life throws at you. Whether it's insisting on a better table when the restaurant thrusts you to a dank corner just because you're dining alone; or whether it's dealing with having your purse pinched on the streets of New York, the-I-can-do-it experience is one that never leaves you. Yes, you can do it. And you don't need a man to do it for you.

Here are some women who discovered elements to their lives they never knew existed until they were single.

Flying Solo

Mostly, thinking about having a partner just wore off. And that was helped by doing things I would just like to do. After doing some career-development training in the US, I hired a van and went off travelling on my own. Travelling is something I love to do. I went off round the Far East with my first boyfriend. When I was thinking about driving around America alone, I realized *ideally* I'd like to be doing it with a partner, but since I wasn't with a partner, I'd do it anyway. Things like that were big transitions for me. I was quite nervous about it beforehand, but mainly I realized that was about doing something stupid on the roads because I was in a big machine on strange roads in America. But actually as soon as I got behind the wheel, the thrill was instant. I hadn't even got out of the garage. When I climbed in, it was *oh yess*, this is really great. And driving along I thought this feels great whether I'm with someone or not.

That's when I knew I was single. I wasn't missing a partner. I was just thinking, 'Oh I'm doing this thing that normally I would do with a partner'. It felt massively single to do in a really affirming way. It was great.

Sarah

While I was single I was working for a travel firm, and I got to go to all sorts of places I'd never afford to go to otherwise, just because I could drop everything and go whenever a trip was offered. When you have a partner you just can't do that. You have to check with them; you have to watch your holiday time so you make sure you spend the right amount with them. I remember sitting in a little beach hut on Bali, thinking I'd never have got here with a partner, and I wouldn't have it any other way.

Jacqui

The best day of my life was a day I spent on my own when I was single. It was exciting, and up until then I had always thought exciting would be something I'd do with someone else.

I was travelling in Malaysia and I'd arranged to meet another couple and do this journey to a national park together, but they didn't turn up. But I'd made the booking so I set off, and I didn't know where I was going to end up. I had this extraordinary journey which was absolutely thrilling and I didn't know what would be beyond the next corner at any point.

I got a bus ride to a boat, I got the wrong boat but it turned out it was the best one because it was very slow. It was me and this one man steering this very low powered engine, zigzagging across a wide river. It was very dramatic and like being in a film. I saw an island ahead and thought, is this the place we're going but it obviously wasn't and we coasted along through mangrove swamps and every now and then fishing boats would pass and people would wave and I thought God this is extraordinary. Then I thought, really I'm taking a bit of a risk; this man might turn the boat and rape me, then I thought, oh well, I don't think he'll do that.

The beauty of it was just amazing. And I was struggling with this narrative in my head. Part of my brain was constantly trying to imagine how I'd describe all this to friends when I got back. Then I realized this was distracting me from enjoying it here and now, so I would sit on that bit of me and think, just experience this. While I was turning it into words, the bit that was experiencing it was shut down.

So, it was just me with these thoughts, trying not think too much and enjoy the beauty of it all. Finally we glided through a mangrove swamp and I'd arrived.

Louise

I went camping alone and that was a very big thing for me. Especially because somehow camping in the past for me had been all about the excitement of doing it with a partner. At first I was quite frightened because it wasn't a huge campsite and there was no one else there and I felt very alone. I got quite upset because it was dark when I arrived and I got lost down a country lane. I'd always been there before with an ex-boyfriend who'd been a boy scout. I had to put up my own tent in the dark and blow up my own lilo – all that felt like the biggest step towards self-sufficiency. When I finally got the tent all set up I cried for about three hours. Then next morning I woke up there and it was beautiful, covered in dew, and I walked to the sea and spent the day on the beach on my own and it was bliss.

Leah

A big shift happened for me when I decided to drive down to the seaside for a day on my own in winter. I love the sea, but, living in the city, I don't get to see enough of it. Usually in the past I've persuaded boyfriends to go with me. But this time, when I became single, I thought, Why not do it on my own? So I took a thermos, and the dog – did all the things I'd do if someone were with me. And walking the dog and having a cream tea on my own made the place feel so much bigger. Now I know there are experiences I can have on my own that are more powerful than with other people. Before that I would never have thought of just going off to the country for a day in winter on my own. Yet the thought of doing it with a lover would have been romantic. But the buzz I got from doing it alone was enormous.

Rachel

I remember one Christmas going to a rash of work production parties. It was the day before Christmas Eve, and I was going to the last one, due to start at six o'clock. I got all dressed up, caught the 38 bus into London, then I thought, I really don't want to do this. I can't face talking to all those people yet again. So I asked myself what I felt like doing, and just then the bus turned right and went past a cinema and I hopped off and went and watched *101 Dalmations* on my own. The cinema was full of children and me, the only adult there who wasn't a parent. It was fantastic. It felt naughty and silly and fun.

Maria

The biggest single single thrill of all for me was getting a flat of my own – that felt such a huge achievement – choosing somewhere, financing somewhere, actually moving in – all on my own. Then realizing that if I wanted fake fur worktops – and I could afford them – I could have them. With no one to say I couldn't. I immediately painted the living room bright red. Because I wanted to. And because I could.

Rosa

How to Make the Most of it

- To make the most of being single, you do have to become an expert planner. As Maria puts it: 'Being single makes you super efficient at planning, but that's nice too because you're planning fun stuff. I made bloody sure I was doing nice things, because a weekend is incredibly precious. All you have to do is pick up the phone and arrange something to be on. I have a very close family and so whenever I had a weekend where I didn't have plans with friends I could go and hang out with my sister, her two cats and her boyfriend. I was never unwillingly alone. But I was often willingly alone.

  'If I was by myself I'd just paint a picture or do something that made me feel it was time well spent. The one time recently I sat here pissed off and depressed it was waiting for a date to turn up. I played patience. It's ironic – if I'd not been waiting for a man, I'd have done something more exciting than that!'

- Make that extra effort. And you do have to make an extra effort when doing things alone. It doesn't at first feel like the exciting adventure it can become when two of you do it. Then it creeps up on you that there's a different feeling when you make the effort to do something you love, something you chose, just for you. A kind of naughty excitement emerges, along with the thought, no one knows I'm doing this. You have to try it for yourself.
- Bear in mind it can take a while to start appreciating the single state, and don't give up. As Therese explains: 'I get in the car at the end of the salsa class and I used to say to myself you're a sad bastard for going home alone. Then one day I checked with myself and I said, "Actually, I've had a lot of fun". And I got home and I was starving and I had brown toast with marmalade in bed and I thought, "This is great"'.
- Making the most of it is also about making yourself matter. If you plan a day out, then the day arrives and you just don't feel like it, put it off for a week. Be easy on yourself. The point is to nurture the relationship with yourself, not to become your own army general sending yourself out on 'manoeuvres'.

Making The Most Of Your Time Involves Saying 'No' To What You Don't Want

When you're single all manner of people will invite you to do all manner of things. Many of which you won't fancy but you may find it difficult to say no. But, remember, the ability to say no is an important relationship skill, and if you can't do it, you will find yourself with worse repercussions than spending a boring Sunday in a work colleague's garden nursing a glass of warm white wine.

However, saying no to boring Sundays is a good place to practise.

Assertiveness training, which teaches the art of saying no, works on two counts:

- Firstly, remembering your rights. That, for example, you have the right to state your own needs and set your own priorities as a person independent of any roles you might assume in life. (i.e. you have the right to rest on a Sunday rather than go to the boss's garden just because he's your boss).

  Also, you have the right to say no – to anything.

  Plus the right to deal with others without being dependent on them for your approval. If your friend disapproves of you because you don't want to go clubbing with her, it's not your fault.

- Secondly, when the time comes to actually say no, you must choose a statement and stick with it. Do not let yourself be hooked into argument or manipulation. Just keep saying no – what assertiveness training calls the 'broken record' technique – until the other person is sick of hearing it. For example: 'Thanks for asking me to go clubbing but I really need to take it easy this weekend'.

Yes, some occasions will be harder to say no to than others, but making the most of being single does not involve wasting your very precious time.

What To Do...

Plan a whole day's date with yourself. Go for a day out to the seaside, or visit that art gallery you've been meaning to see.

Is there somewhere you'd secretly like to go? Do a bit of research. Find out what happens in your local area at weekends. Plan a trip alone. The scarier the better. Remember the 'Feel the fear' statement: Whatever happens, I'll handle it.

You can try a serious day, like buying the serious Sunday papers and really getting to grips with what's happening in the world. Or have a whole frivolous day and book yourself a massage, a swim, a facial…

Start gently at first, experiment with eating in a restaurant alone by, say, having a coffee alone first.

Of course if you're allergic to solitude you don't have to go it alone. You can still think of what you'd like to do, then see if you can persuade a friend. Or the two of you could daydream together about things that would be fun.

Even if you hate it and decide that for you being a couch potato is where your single life is at, at least you know that and have discovered that *for yourself*.

CHAPTER 10

Friendships in the Single World
5 Ways Friendships Change

You feel better when you surround yourself with people who are like you, in the same position as you; that is, single. So you need to balance the time you spend with certain groups of your friends. Couples and singles. You don't abandon people obviously. But I find myself spending a lot more time with single women I know, and we've become more of a group. They're slightly younger than me too, but we go out and have a great time. I feel really good about myself with them. It's about feeling part of the pack and the same as everyone else. When I'm out and about with people I think 'This is great, I'm having a fantastic time and this is what my life is like'. Sometimes I'm with friends with kids and they're arguing with their partner and I think, 'No way would I want to swap my lifestyle for that'.

Jacqui, on the importance of having a single posse

In part one we looked at how friendships change when you split up with someone. They shift again as you negotiate singlehood.

When we become single we change camps. On an obvious basic level, you have more in common now with other single women, other single people, than you had before with couples. Your paired-up friends know this too. Suddenly they have less in common with you. And the mixed feelings this change in perspective brings can create choppy waters which need very careful negotiating.

Both times I've become single after marriage, I've felt like I slipped back a couple of notches in the life stakes. There they are, getting on with the very adult business of living together, being married, raising children. Here I am, back to dating and kissing and what to wear and freedom – things which, no matter how old you are, feel very teenage. To me and to them.

There are two main aspects affecting friendships in the single world: how your friends behave towards you; and how you are with them. Here are a few pointers:

1. Mixed emotions

All this means you and your hitched friends may now regard one another with a bitter-sweet blend of envy and pity. Lia, a hairdresser, says: 'I find some of my married friends are very smug and patronizing. I went out with two of them the other night and, as I went off to get a drink, I heard one of them say to the other: "Wouldn't it be terrible to have no husband to go home to." I was so furious I nearly thumped her.'

Yes, married friends may pity you. They may also secretly envy your glamorous, exciting unfettered existance. Part of the problem is the two camps – you and them – represent to one another what each doesn't have – and might miss. Your fixed-up friends can't go out and dance like a slut, clamp lips with four different men of an evening then stagger home at four in the morning. At least, not without the Spanish Inquisition. And you can't do cosy cuddling up on the sofa on a Friday night.

Lia is not single by choice and part of her fury about her friend's remark is because it struck an envious chord. This is the very reason you may find being with couples positively off-putting. They remind you of what you're not.

As one 34-year-old singleton puts it:

Recently I went out with several couples and me, and although it was a great evening, I did feel slightly deflated going home, because I was in company of all couples. It was partly because I was thinking they're all paired off and that's what I want and I'm not having what I want and why haven't I got that; and also, I suppose, feeling different and a bit abnormal for my age. So I do tend to steer clear of evenings like that because it doesn't make me feel good. You spend time with people who have a completely different lifestyle with kids and you get a bit kidded out. So although I don't want to give up seeing my couple friends and I do do it, I also need to do the things that are more similar to me and make me feel normal and not such a freak.

The major factor which definitely puts a bridge between you and the couples of this world is children, and the overwhelming effect they have on people's lives. Being around small people may bring up painful feelings if your biological clock is on overdrive. As Louise, solo for seven years, puts it: 'I have found it difficult when friends have had babies because to me that represents the ultimate commitment. Someone has loved that woman enough to want a baby with her and here it is, miraculous living proof of that fact. I can't even get a date at the moment, let alone be fertilized. So seeing babies always makes me a bit teary and makes some people hard to visit.'

If they're really good friends, and big enough to take it, confiding your envious feelings can really help them disappear. No one who hears you talk from the heart about how seeing children makes you sad about what what you're missing, can fail to be moved by it.

2. Fixing you up

No one likes to feel there's anything 'wrong' with the way they live their life. So the other thing that can be testing is the way couples continually try to get you back into the couples camp. As Louise says: 'I've had good relationships with several old boyfriends – we have kept up a loving contact – so it's always been slightly difficult when they get the wife. What I can't bear is people worrying about me. I can't bear to be with one old boyfriend and his wife because they always want to fix me up. The attitude is poor old Louise what can we do for her. I feel like saying just enjoy me when you invite me round for dinner and not try and sort me out, that's what you can do for me.'

Alternatively, your single state becomes partnered-up with people's entertainment as they vicariously live out through you the roller-coaster ride of their own single years. This can also be trying. 'You can tend to be the entertainment in an "Oooh, what's going on then?" way. And that's kind of annoying. And you tell them and they tease you about it like it's a big laugh when actually you may feel very vulnerable about it all.'

This is also Emily's experience. She says: 'You get some people who are really uncomfortable with their single friends and try and pair you off. And that's very annoying for the single person. It's like you're not anyone if you're on your own. But I think single people should feel smug because no one wakes up in the morning and thinks, I'm so happy, everyone should be this happy. It stems from a kind of envy.'

You don't have to entertain married friends with every detail of your freedom years, unless you want to.

3. Leaving you out

Some people are so committedly couply they can alienate single friends by treating them like pariahs. As Leah puts it 'I was treated differently by married people when I was single. One friend I'd had for years never invited me to a dinner party but would invite people she hardly knew, and that really hurt. It's like the time of the bloody ark. I don't think society makes it easy for single people.'

So either you're not invited along to couply fixtures or you are and you feel like a spare part; or they try and fix you up with some appalling no-hoper and sit there hawk-like all night for any glimmers of attraction.

What can be worst of all though, is when one of your single friends jumps camp and, just like a highly priced footballer who swaps teams, starts pretending they never had anything to do with the old lot.

Emily says:

My very best friend for 18 years dumped me the minute she met someone. It was astonishing. We went from phoning one another every day to not phoning at all. That was gutting. I felt hideously sorry for myself. I had a double loss to deal with because I didn't have someone and she did, and I didn't have her. When she announced her engagement I cried in front of her, and she said, 'Emily, getting married is what people do in their twenties.' It was a selfish, smug thing to say, that threw my situation into relief.

4. Women behaving badly

But the bad behaviour is not all on one side. Singles are quite capable of it too.

After the above experience, Emily did a little stropping herself:

When my other really good friend met someone at university, we had this huge, horrible row. Because she was in a relationship and I wasn't, I acted towards her like she owed me, emotionally. It was as if because she was happy I felt I could be a bit of a brat because I deserved pity. I know a lot of people who do this. I have a single friend who isn't a good friend to her best friend any more, now that the best friend has a boyfriend. She expects her to pick her up and take her places. It's like her attitude is: 'She's got everything and I haven't and she owes me'.

Of course this doesn't happen with everyone. I have friends who are couples who I adore and look forward to seeing with just as much enthusiasm as when I was one of them.

But weird things can happen to friendships and it's good to be aware. Because, when you're on your own problems with friends can leave you feeling extra isolated. It can help to know it's a common experience – it's not just you.

Is your best friend becoming your relationship substitute?

It can happen that you transfer all your partnering energy onto the next best option in your life, your best mate. You can find yourself getting all het up when she doesn't behave like a boyfriend, or gets one herself. If you find the relationship becoming more tense – you start having tantrums, fights, conflict – ask yourself whether you're looking to her for everything. But bear in mind that it's OK to have some conflict, and that all this is practice in the art of *relating*, which you can practise every day, with everyone from the milkman to your mother. Also remember you don't want to alienate your friend if she is a good friend.

5. Creating a single posse

If your relationship with coupled friends has taken a slight turn for the worse, there are compensations. You join a new club called 'single people' where an integral part of the membership contract is to lighten up and have fun.

The answer, then, is to create a single posse.

Hopefully, by now, you have created your own support network. You know who supports you and who doesn't. You also need a single posse. Even if it's only two of you. But the more the merrier. Single women hunt in packs.

You may join an existing single posse. You may have to create your own.

Of course, you may need a whole new social life to replace sitting on the sofa on a Saturday night.

You need to talk to other singles about what it's like. If you hardly know any other single people, try singles nights, not just to meet men, but to meet *friends*. The less friends you have, the more likely you are to fall into the 'I need a man to make my life all right' trap.

When you're single, you inevitably spend more time with your female friends, and many single women mention how this is one of the unexpected benefits of single status. Like Rachel, who says:

There was definitely a turning point in my life when I realized the value of women friends. I've come to realize I had categorized a relationship with a man out of context, as if that was the only relationship that would give me what I needed. So before, I didn't find all female contact enjoyable and I needed a man in order to have an interesting time. Now I find being with women is fantastic because we're on the same wavelength. We're able to discuss feminity and how we get on together without being competitive over a man. That's given me a sense of identity and belonging. In a man's world women often feel they have to be part of the world by being attached to a man. I feel there is a woman's world which is always there. I have found a lot of the emotional support and closeness I look for in a relationship in women friends. If you have a network of female friends you're not so needy when with a man. And that actually puts you in a stronger position to have a relationship with a man.

The virtues of a messed-up mate

On the other hand, the final word on friendship in the single word has to come from Ella, who extols the great virtue of having a friend whose love life is in a worse state than yours is. She says:

It's important to have a friend who has an even worse love life than you. No matter how many bastards you date, she dates more. No matter how much weight you put on, she puts on more. Someone who makes you think, oh well, at least my life's not that bad.

Bear in mind, though, that if you have to feel this way – pleased that someone else is worse off than you – you are not exactly single and loving it. It sounds like you're single and miserable…

Pointers To Help Fast Friendships

- Have a different attitude when you're with couples. If you start to feel a little unloved, remember that it's only for an evening. Jacqui advises, 'Maybe it only gets to you when you think "that's what I want". I don't always allow myself to think this because what is the point in focussing on something you don't have. It's just depressing. I say work with what you have got. Have a focus.'
- Remember, you don't have to do anything you don't want to do or go anywhere you don't want to go. One time I was due to go to a friend's baby's christening when I was having a very down patch. I found myself feeling incredibly anxious about it, so I did something

different – I called my friends, explained exactly how I was feeling, and asked if I could just go to the party rather than the ceremony. Much as I loved them, I just couldn't face a concentrated burst of couply celebration. And my friends were lovely and supportive and I felt a hundred times better. This kind of asking for what you want, and getting it, is good practice at the tricky business of relating.

- Spending time with children is an excellent cure for broodiness. Think how the harassed mother feels when you walk out back to a nice hot bath or nice hot date and she goes back to peeling nice hot dinner off her nice hot neck.
- You have to be grown up about it, and keep telling yourself your time will come. Times like this really test your positive thinking.
- Make new friends. Join a gym. Or a singles club. The myth that old friends are best friends and new ones just won't be the same is just that, a myth. We all change and as we do different people come into our lives who relate to the new parts of ourselves.
- It's good to do things regularly. Like Friday night girls' night in watching *Friends* and *Frasier*. That way you know you won't be alone all week.
- Be proactive. Suggest you and the girls go someplace.
- Be honest with people. Tell them what you need. Exaggerate it to make it lighter. 'Look, I really *need* this! (company, a hug, help moving house) I'm desperate!'

Exercise

Draw a circle in your journal. Put outside it friends who don't support your single self. Inside it write the names of friends who do support your single self.

Now, who you gonna call?

Ignore advice
Don't listen to friends telling you what to do. A lot of it is their stuff:
'You don't need a man' or...
'When are you going to find someone to make you happy.'
'What do you mean you've chucked him? He was gorgeous.'
Learn to listen to your own wisdom. And if you make mistakes, so what. You made a mistake and mistakes are what we learn from.

When Sally Met Harry – The Joys Of A Male Friend

I really recommend having a male girlfriend. Pete was like a surrogate boyfriend. He was instrumental in introducing me to the concept of going out and having a good time and not caring what anyone thought. He seemed incredibly well connected and could always get us in to whatever hot party was happening. He was a complete hedonist and conveniently knew lots of other spunky men who seemed appropriately impressed with my age and experience (I was a little bit older than most of them). So we spent the next two years getting off with each other's friends.

Ella, 26

One excellent arena for practising relationships while not 'in' one, is to have male friends. Some women have an abundance of male friends quite naturally. Other women find they don't have any – men are either authority figures, work colleagues or people they have sex with.

Even if you do have male 'girlfriends', you may not treat them exactly the same as you do your women friends. You may find you have a jokey, flirty, or intellectual relationship with them, but you save the real emotional sharing for women.

But men have feelings too. And sharing feelings with a man you don't fall in love with is a wonderful, non-threatening arena to practise being real in relationships.

Benefits:

- He can give you the male perspective on what went wrong in your past relationship, why the current one hasn't phoned or whether you come across to men as attractive, reserved, over-assertive etc…

- You learn more about how men think and feel. He may tell you things maybe a partner in a relationship wouldn't.
- You practise being with a man in a different, non-sexual way. This can help break patterns of acting differently, and therefore unnaturally, around men, or of sexual addiction.

Leah gained enormous benefits from her 'honorary girlfriend'.

We did an evening class together, a life drawing class. He wasn't a big friend then but I mentioned I was going to do the class and he really wanted to too. So we were seeing each other every week at the class, then he split with his girlfriend and I wasn't going out with anyone, so we started to just turn into people who did things together. The thing I like about men friends is they like doing *things. With my girlfriends we sit around each others' houses and hang out and chat, whereas he'll suggest sailing on his friend's boat.*

We got to be very good friends. Before, when I used to be not going out with someone, I always filled the gap a boyfriend left with a 'special' man – like a flatmate; or a guy I went round with all the time – they were very much boyfriend substitutes. That was definitely my way of having what you have from a relationship. But Jeremy was different. I remember thinking 'I can treat him like a man' – which for me meant someone I can't quite be the same as with a woman, or can let slip into the woman category. What was hard to let go of, even though I didn't fancy him, was, because he was a man and eligible, I had to somehow make an effort to be a perfect woman in front of him. The watershed came when we went camping together. I went without makeup, I didn't wash my hair, I even peed in front of him! All those things you wouldn't think twice about doing with a girlfriend. It was a big step in not treating men as these separate, special human beings you have to put on a big performance for. My friendship with Jeremy was valuable practice at becoming more real around men.

Similarly, Therese says of her honorary girlfriend, Sam: 'He's been wonderful. I've talked a lot with him about what's happened with me around men and it's been so good to get a male perspective.'

Of course, sex can rear its head. You may find yourself falling for him (in which case, *see page 237*) or he may fall for you. This happened to Therese. She said: 'Sam and I have been friends for years, and when I became single he began to get a bit possessive around me. He took me to a family party and it was obvious he hadn't told people I wasn't his girlfriend. So I sat him down and said, "You're lovely. You know I really care about you. But you and I don't have a future together."'

And – who knows? – maybe one day you'll find that, like when Harry met Sally, you two are destined to be.

And maybe you won't, but you'll have gained enormously anyway.

CHAPTER 11

Mapping Your Patterns

When I was thinking about my family history and the messages I got growing up, one thing I realized was that in my family a woman without a man was regarded as some kind of freak. She was seen as someone nobody wanted. So I was brought up to believe a woman should be with a man.

As a result, rather than talking me out of marrying at 18, my father said that, as I was the youngest daughter, he could rest on his laurels now, his work was done.

The other thing that dawned on me about my family was that all the women in my family were carers before anything else. They stopped working once they had someone to care for. Consequently, as each of my relationships finished, I went in search of someone else to care for. This behaviour always found me partners who needed a lot of investment, and who didn't know how to give back to me. They were too needy themselves to have anything left over. Now I know to look for someone who's going to be there for me too and not accept anything less.

Therese, on what she discovered by mapping patterns in her own life

If you are to truly recover from a broken relationship and make the most of being single, it's crucial to understand what went wrong with relationships in the past. Maybe you haven't had any relationships yet; maybe you've had several. Either way, and even if what just ended was a happy successful relationship that just fizzled out, we can always learn more about ourselves, fascinating creatures that we are.

Relationships are always where we learn most. They tell us enormous amounts about our attitude towards ourselves and other people, our strengths and character flaws, our level of self-worth. And information is power. Once you see the patterns weaving through the tapestry of your life you can start to choose a design of your own.

Taking a cool, honest look at our patterns helps us take responsibility for ourselves and our part in the relationship dynamic. It can throw up hidden parts of ourselves and is wonderful for helping us forgive our ex and move on. This is the part where you save yourself a bundle in therapist's fees, and do the job yourself.

Breaking up is hard to do. It's not an event any of us would willingly enter into again in life's Olympics. Next time, I'm sure, you'd rather opt for the relationship marathon (preferably one which only ends when one of the two competitors conks out at the age of 103, not when they bowl out half way through) than a short sprint followed by yet another dose of pain.

Fortunately there's something you can do right now to bring that dream of a loving, happy, long-lasting relationship closer. And which will have the added payoff of helping you feel better about yourself in the short-term.

All it takes is a little private detective work on what went wrong to make sure you don't make the same mistakes again. The following questions contribute to the crucial business of self-awareness. With awareness you can make a choice as to whether you want to repeat patterns again. Without awareness you're destined to boing through life like the silver sphere in a pinball machine, ricocheting from one rubber-hubbed disaster to the next.

Past Relationships Checklist

Use these prompts to mull over your relationship history. It helps enormously to write your responses down in your feelings journal. If you really hate writing, think about these things, then make a time to talk about all this with your closest friend (or some other trusted person).

Later on we'll talk about what some of these answers *mean*...

What was my ex-partner like?
What did I find most attractive about him/her?
What was it I couldn't stand by the end?

Do my ex-partners have anything in common?
If so what? Think about:
Positive aspects (charming, handsome, funny, kind, generous, artistic, intelligent)
Negative aspects (unreliable, unavailable, workaholic, drank too much, cold, unemotional, critical, angry, indecisive)

Why did it end?
Who ended it?
For what reason?
Have other relationships finished in the same way?
Would you have ended it anyhow?
Did you manifest a crisis to get what you secretly wanted?

How was I in the relationship?
What did I do that contributed to the break-up? (Remember, this is just information to help you, *not* to be used as ammunition to beat yourself up with)

Did I do any of the following:

Bottle my anger up so it turned into resentment so my love just died
Keep losing my temper so it turned him against me
Allow myself to be bullied, put down or criticised (about my body, my intelligence, my personality, my lifestyle)
Believe my partner must always be right – and act accordingly

Endure infidelity
Be unfaithful myself
Avoid intimacy by refusing to share my deepest thoughts and feelings with him
Be always looking for the one thing that would make it work
Focus on him and what he wanted at the expense of myself and what I wanted
Criticize/nag him
Do things he wanted to do at the expense of what I wanted to do
Be always the one to initiate displays of affection
Ignore signs the relationship wasn't working
Indulge any addictions like overeating or excessive drinking
or anything else that didn't make you feel good about yourself and him?

The point of this exercise is to:
Bust through any dreamy denial that, really, it was a fabulous relationship, really it was; to help you notice it takes two to tango and realize you are the only person whose actions can bring change into your life.

What was the payoff for me in my last relationship or series of relationships?
Did I:

Get to stay stuck and not have to change
Get to stay a child and be looked after and be dependent
Get my own need to be needed met by mothering him
Get my own need to be superior met by his lack of responsibility
Get to avoid my own problems by focussing on him
Get someone financially secure to help pay for me/my children?

What do my friends/family say about my relationships?
Think about the feedback friends and family have given you about your last relationship, or last series of relationships. Bear in mind that some of it may fall into the category of 'their stuff', i.e. coloured by their own beliefs and opinions about the way you should live your life. But these *are* the people who know you best and you'd be mad not to take note of any common themes. Especially ponder the remarks that annoy you the most – they're often ones with a kernel of truth we don't want to look at. (Don't worry, they need never know they were even the teeniest bit right!)

Was he like daddy?

Or mummy? Or a brother or sister, uncle, aunt, favourite schoolteacher, your first love?

This is where we're indulging in a little self-therapy. You can save yourself hours in a shrink's office (not to mention pounds in your purse) by noticing patterns in your partner or relationship that reflect patterns in the family you grew up in. (All will be explained later.)

What was our sex life like?

Did either of you go off sex?

Did you have difficulties, like impotence on his side or lack of lubrication on yours?

Or one of you being keener than the other?

When did any difficulties begin, or did you have sexual problems/issues from the outset?

Our sex life is often a very accurate thermometer for reading the health of a love relationship. Problems and conflicts have a habit of showing up here before anywhere else. Although, sometimes, great sex can be a way of maintaining a kind of intimacy when everything else is drifting.

OK, Here Comes The Science...

Relationship history has a habit of repeating itself. We tend to attract the same kinds of people over and over. That's what's meant by relationship patterns.

There are certain loops women fall into with men. If they're positive – you always choose men who love, cherish you, and treat you like a princess – no problem. It's the negative patterns that get us mired in misery.

Common negative patterns include repeatedly hooking up with:

Emotionally unavailable men – cold, distant, possibly over-focussed on other activities like work

Little boys – won't take responsibility for anything and you end up mothering them

Father figures – can be overly protective so you end up feeling stifled

A challenge – hard work, or unavailable, and you exhaust yourself trying to relate to them

Need rescuing – helpless, too shy, bad with money

Big rescuers – are great when you're in a crisis but thereafter try to control you by telling you what to do

Controlling men – bossy, domineering, won't let you live your own life

Addicted men – to drink, drugs, sex or some other substance, maybe even work

Abusive men – verbally, physically or sexually
Unfaithful men/womanizers – need I say more?
Commitment-phobes – adore women, desperately desire contact but won't go the distance
Violent men

Was He Like Daddy?

What has *he* got to do with it? Plenty. There is abundant evidence that family patterns repeat themselves. It was Freud who first said that a child's early upbringing in their first family influences the whole of the rest of their lives. Since then, whatever else they disagree with him about, psychologists concur that on this point he was bang to rights.

We learn about relationships at mummy and daddy's knees. And from that unfortunate vantage point our parents seem like gods – they must be right, we decide, because we know no different and they seem all-powerful. So, we learn from them what 'love' is. We learn from our father what men are like. We learn from our mother how women relate to men. Daddy might be a terrible shyster and mummy no role model, but we don't know that. It all seeps into our subconscious and lodges in the file marked 'love'. And it's tragically obvious that if, say, what is presented to us as love is actually something cold and hard, we will go for cold, hard lovers every time.

People who grow up in happy, secure homes abundant with love and affection and where the children are allowed to be themselves are the lucky ones. The rest of us have what psychologists call 'issues' to deal with.

My own example gives you a good idea what 'issues' can be like:

All the time I was growing up – an only child – my father ignored me.

I never once had a family holiday with him, never went to the park, never played ball; he never helped me with my reading, or tucked me into bed. He would eat in another room, except for excruciating family lunches, him sitting with his back to me, eating as though under prison warder's orders, then getting up as soon as he could. I would then heave a sigh of relief. My tactic, the defense mechanism I developed for dealing with this, was to ignore him back. Hard.

Now I am older, I realize he was clinically depressed. His own childhood was terrible. Beaten by his drunken father, shut in closets. He tried to be as unlike his father as possible. And he was. He never drank. And rather than the unwanted attention violence represents, he substituted no attention at all.

When I left home at 17, I believed I had reached adulthood unscathed. I was wrong.

I have mapped my own patterns and the effects of having a father who ignored me have been profound. I have been fatally attracted to men who weren't wholly available. Mostly they've been workaholics – just like daddy. Certainly there's always been some challenge, some way of having to work hard to gain their attention. Not always successfully. Until recently the idea of a nice, loving, available man has seemed deathly dull. My rebound relationship man was more like my father than any man before or since. It was as though I couldn't resist one more crack at a man just like daddy. But this time there was a difference. It just didn't feel OK. I knew I deserved better and I could let it – and hopefully that whole pattern – go. Finally, after 20-odd years of grappling with it.

A healthy relationship with her father is important for a girl. Without it, she may be condemned to search for it in all the wrong places.

My story is fairly typical of women who've had some kind of childhood unhappiness. If we grow up with difficulties in our crucial primary relationships, we're presented with a double-edged sword with two consequences likely to affect our adult love relationships:

We Find Ourselves Attracted To People Who Resemble Our Parents/Siblings

Don't ask me why, but virtually all of my serious relationships have been with Librans. Dark-haired, chisel-cheeked

Librans at that. And my first-ever serious relationship, some 20 years ago now, was with – yes – a raven-haired, chisel-cheeked, kiss-me-I'm-gorgeous Libran.

At the same time those same Librans have had an unfortunate tendency to be emotionally cold and somehow unavailable. Just like daddy.

Psychologists say that, from an early age, we create romantic lovemaps. That our past experiences with people who have loved us, or – even – didn't love us, prompt us to fashion identikit pictures of the type of person we find attractive. The qualities in our lovemaps are not just physical but emotional and psychological too.

Lovemaps reside in our unconscious. We never *say*, right, now I'll go after another emotionally unavailable, Spurs-mad Volvo-driver with a hairy chest. But isn't it weird how we can spot a stranger across a crowded room, only to discover later, when we have a peep, that not only does he have a hairy chest and a cool demeanour, but – bloody hell – he drools over Spurs as well. Then if we ponder a little about our dad, brother or the boy next door we're bound to uncover some familiar factors. Like maybe daddy loved Spurs and large Swedish cars.

Of course, these are silly examples. Yours are bound to be much subtler and much more fascinating. But you get the drift. And once you consider your own psychological patterns – what was the pay-off for me in this relationship? You can see what you were getting. This will highlight needs in you that you might address yourself while you're single.

As a Cosmo feature once said: Your type may not *be* your type. The one that makes your heart zing, your eyes tingle and your loins boggle – the one who lights up your love map – may well not be the one you could happily spend the rest of your life with.

We Constantly Repeat Patterns Because We Are Trying To Heal Old Traumas

It's like our subconscious thinks: 'If I get this bullying, critical man to love me maybe it will make up for how bullying, critical daddy never loved me and I will, at last, have got what I'm searching for'. Except, of course, bullying critical men just keep on being what they are – critical bullies – and once again we're broken-hearted.

This explains why women from homes where one or both parents were alchoholic have a tragic tendency to hook up with alchoholic partners; why women who've been hit as children tend to gravitate towards men who end up hitting them. Shrinks call this habit of re-creating the dynamic experienced with a difficult parent 'repetition compulsion'.

So, it's worth asking yourself:

What was my relationship with my father like?
What was my relationship with my mother like?
Ditto for any siblings?
Have I had any past experiences which are influencing my present relationships in a negative way?
How do I feel about men?
Am I acting out a repetition compulsion, and if so what is it?

Notice whether your last relationship demonstrated an improvement on the ones before or a step down on a slippery slope. If gorgeous no-goods are your thing, was he more or less of a gorgeous no-good than the one before? If he was an improvement – hooray! If a slip back, well, c'est la vie. Life has a habit of making certain things we need to notice bigger and bigger until we can no longer run from what's in front of our face. Dust yourself off and start again.

CHAPTER 12

Busting the Beliefs

I always had a core belief I was thick and ugly and not desirable and not lovable. And I've really had to discover that thing everyone says about loving yourself. It's only as I've actually started to consciously have more belief in myself that the way I feel about myself has improved. It's quite hard to love yourself unless you start finding your path at the same time. It's hard to draw out the strands. Going to art college helped me lose that belief. I wasn't looking only for satisfaction and approval from other people, I was getting it from myself in a way. The process of art is all very much about putting your insides out there anyway.

Leah, on the advantages of busting negative beliefs

One more question to ask yourself:

What messages did I get growing up, from family, my environment, society, even film, TV and magazines about love and relationships?

As Therese's testimony, which began the last chapter, illustrates, family messages are powerful. Think about not just how your parents behaved, but what they said to you.

My mother stayed all her married life in a difficult, draining, destructive relationship with my father until he died, when she blossomed. It was her choice to stay with him and her prerogative. And it offered me the unspoken, unconscious message that any old relationship is better than none. (Let's be clear, I'm not blaming her here, just illustrating how we glean information that will help us create a happier future.)

The repercussions of absorbing this message in my life have been: firstly, that I have spent a great deal of my life in relationships; secondly that when I did leave a relationship that was not working it felt very scary indeed; thirdly, that I find it a real challenge to not have anyone, even when I know I need to be alone. I'm not proud of this, but it's easier for me to be kind to myself about it when I remind myself I am grappling with a powerful, ancient, family pattern.

As we go about our everyday life, that file in our subconscious marked 'love' gets fatter and fatter, as it is constantly updated. It gets filled from an early age with happy-ever-after fairy stories, which may blatantly contradict what we know about love from our parents' divorce. It gets filled when we observe what 'love' means to our parents, our grandparents, our friends' parents' relationships. It gets added to when we start kissing boys – getting our hearts broken and breaking other hearts. It gets added to every time we watch a soppy movie.

Here's an exercise for opening that file and having a peep at the contents right at the bottom of the barrel.

Those dusty, dog-eared shreds at the bottom of the heap which, laid down years ago, may still be the major dictators to our happy hearts: they are our deepest beliefs.

Exercise

Make a list of the beliefs about relationships you grew up with using the cues below. They will illustrate your relationship belief system which you are acting out in your everyday life.

Some examples…

All men are bastards

Other women aren't to be trusted

Nobody can be trusted

He'll leave you in the end

It's crucial to be married

When I'm married, I'll be happy

I can't be happy on my own

It's better to stay in a crappy relationship than be alone on a Saturday night

I must have someone's total attention all of the time in order to believe they love me

If someone loves you, they never want to spend time with anyone else

I must always look good and be nice in order for a man to love me

No one will love me if they see what I'm really like
I'm only OK if someone loves me
I can't cope on my own
I am responsible for everyone else's feelings
I'm nothing without a man
Sex equals love
I am basically incompetent and incapable and I need some-one to look after me
Men should always earn more money than women
I don't deserve to be loved in the way I would like
I'm crap with men
I must always be right and never make a mistake
What other people do is vitally important to me, and I should make every effort to change them into what I want them to be

Think also about how your parents behaved and what beliefs they might have acted out. Talk to them – people's basic beliefs often come out in their speech without their realizing it. Comments like 'That's just men, they're all babies' betrays a belief that all men are basically immature, incompetent no-hopers and women are superior.

You'll discover that some of your beliefs may be perfectly fine and dandy – like, everyone should be treated with respect. And some may be, at best, dodgy. Others are likely to be real doozies.

My beliefs about men are...
My beliefs about women are...

The message about men I got from my mother is...
The message about men I got from my father is...
The message about women I got from my father is...
The message about women I got from my mother is...
The message about sex I got from my parents is...
The message about love I got from my parents is...
The beliefs my childhood experiences tend to give me about men/love are...
The beliefs my adolescent experiences tend to give me about men/love/sex are...
The beliefs my adult experiences tend to give me about men/love/sex are...

Then think about grandparents, step-parents, siblings, aunts, uncles, schoolteachers, significant friends, nannies. What did they tell you about love, men, women, relationships?

Try and identify a core belief which feels stronger than all the rest, or which encapsulates many of your attitudes.

Then ask yourself the all-important question:

What is the pay-off for holding on to this belief?

For example, Mary grew up in a family where sex was never talked about except in derogatory terms – by both parents. So she grew up with the message that sex is dirty and somehow wrong. That translated into a belief: Sex is bad. I'm bad if I want it.

The pay off for holding this belief is that Mary has never sustained a loving, long-term relationship, and never truly let go to enjoy the sweet, sassy side of life.

Once again, remember the information you uncover is simply to help you understand yourself. Not to start putting yourself down with.

Beliefs, once unearthed, can be changed. For every doozy you came up with, think of something that would be more positive. Like,

All men are bastards

I choose not to believe this any more. I choose to believe men are basically OK.

I'm crap with men

I choose not to believe this any more. I choose to believe my relationships are getting better and better.

And so on. Once you do this, you're using the very powerful tool of affirmations. By repeating them over and over, they can lead to actions which can bring about the changes you want to bring into your life. Repeat your statements on the bus, in the bath, in your lunchbreak – until they seep into your subconscious love file and replace some of the tatty old rubbish lurking there.

Tips for creating affirmations:

- Keep them in the present tense, as though what you desire is already happening. So not 'One day I will be in a happy, healthy relationship.' But 'I am creating a happy healthy relationship.'

- Accentuate the positive; eliminate the negative. So, don't say: 'I am no longer attracted to unavailable men'. But, 'I am attracted to loving, caring men'.
- Repeat them over and over, pin them on your bedroom wall, say them in the bath, tape them and play them to yourself while driving.
- Back up specific affirmations about what you want with this all-purpose version for dumping the past: 'I release all negative beliefs'.

The All-Crucial Lottery-Winning Question:

What Does All This Tell Me About My Level Of Self-Esteem?

I started to see a counsellor and that gave me the support I needed to build my self-esteem which had been so desperately lacking in my life. I'd kept it hidden extremely well, but it would come out in weird ways, like exercising myself so hard I hurt my knee. Or trying too hard at work because I thought otherwise they wouldn't like me, but I was exhausting myself. And I was always dating men who didn't look after me in any way. It felt more and more like I was on the edge of a chasm. Little bits were always crumbling away and I could fall into it any minute.

In counselling, as I began to look at my relationships with my parents and siblings I stopped trying to date them. Before that, in my single phase, I'd had a short time with a guy who was alcoholic, just like my dad; then a much younger guy who even looked just like my younger brother; then a couple of one night stands with a guy who was achingly like my out-of-it drug-addict sister. It's weird how you're always trying to heal the relationships that never went right in the relationships you get now. But once I realized what I was doing, like magic I met someone who was genuine and caring.

Elaine, 26, on her dating patterns

Self-esteem is a buzz-word these days, for good reason. It *is* crucially important. It's not some sell-by-date trend which, five years on, will be as redundant as last week's latest pop phenomenon. Like organic vegetables and calcium tablets, building our self-worth is something that is genuinely good for us, now and in the future. Self-esteem, as they say in the movies, has legs.

So how is yours doing? Could it do with toning up?

What we're talking about here, basically, is how much we value ourselves. If, deep down, you believe you're not much cop – not pretty, not clever, in some way not loveable – your self-esteem could do with a boost. And don't feel you're on your own. Everyone has different levels of self-worth. Even people who seem to have fame, fortune and the whole damn thing, frequently feel that deep down they're a fraud and one day will be found out.

Equally, we can't expect anyone else to value us if we don't. You wouldn't want to buy a cola from a company which said 'This cola is crap, we put any old rubbish in it, we can't be bothered to sell it properly and we just give it, gratis, to the first one who asks'. You want to buy cola from a company which says 'This is *it*. The real thing'.

As with cola, so with you.

When we behave as though we're not worth much, guess what? We attract people who treat us like we're not worth much.

Self-esteem is a funny thing. You can have it in abundance in some areas of your life and be scraping the barrel in others. Like Therese, whose quote began this chapter. She is one of Britain's leading management consultants and is paid a fortune for helping companies sort their problems out. Yet her insecurity around men has been huge. She could be bolshie in the boardroom yet belittled in bed. Ever since she met her first husband at 16, she has repeatedly hooked up with emotionally unavailable men for whom she has given and given in an attempt to somehow 'prove' herself loveable. At the age of 39, nearly two years into being single, Therese found a breast lump. Fortunately, it was benign. And its repercussions were yet more fortunate. She says: 'Something about having that breast lump made me realize so strongly how I've put up with receiving so little from men. How I've always been with the takers of this world. Now I know I'm going to stay single until I meet someone who values me as much as I value me now.'

You deserve better!

Symptoms of low self-esteem in relationships:

Giving in
Putting up with
Not asking
Asking the impossible
Denying
Excusing/making excuses
Moaning (if it was that bad, and you genuinely believed you deserve better, you'd be off)
Etc etc...

Now ask yourself:

If I really loved myself, if I really valued and respected myself, would I have put up with that?

If I was my own best friend, what would I say to myself?

Tools that improve self-esteem:

Affirmations
Saying no to bad relationships

Taking emotional risks (asking for what you want, telling friends about behaviour you don't like)
Nurturing yourself
Being single and taking your life into your own hands
The independence and control being single can offer

The good, no, exhilarating news is that women who've been single for any length of time found it raised self-esteem and busted old negative or unhelpful patterns (remember the quotes which began Chapter 8?).

Warning – Beware the label

There is a tendency, doing your patterns mapping exercises, to start labelling. To indulge the 'I always go for bastards' syndrome. Not all men are bastards. Not all bastards are bastards. As Susan Jeffers says in her wise book *Opening Our Hearts To Men,* 'We can't blame men for walking all over us, we can only notice we're not moving out of the way.'

This work is simply to build your awareness, not to act as fuel for criticizing yourself or him. You chose him for a reason. There is an abundance of gifts you received from your last partner. Even if it was an awful relationship, maybe the 'awfulness' offered a kind of familiarity. This is useful information – you will know for next time!

Change Something Now!

All of this is pure hogwash if you don't start putting it into practice. Yet when you do, it can genuinely change your life. And there are ways to practise, even without a relationship!

Take the information from your patterns mapping exercise and make small steps. Don't decide, OK, I'm never going to let anyone take advantage of me again. You aren't going to change your personality overnight. What you can do, however, is start in small ways, say, with saying no to a work colleague who is always asking you to do things for him and not letting him take advantage of you. Because, if you noticed in your relationships you didn't stand up for yourself or get what *you* needed, it's likely you do that in other relationships too. So start standing up for yourself with family and close friends. If you gave in too soon, practise being stubborn and do it at work, in your social life, with your family. If you lost your temper too often, try holding your breath and counting to ten the next time someone gets your goat.

Like Ariana who says: 'After splitting up with John, some of my friends said they couldn't believe how controlling he was. And I realized my part in it was I never asked what I wanted, we always did things he wanted to do. So I think he didn't respect me, then walked all over me. And I let him. So, with friends, I started to think, what do I really want to do? And then say it: I want to do so-and-so. Rather than I don't mind, you decide. And, just with that little change, I began to feel so much better – better about myself, and happier. Now I know I won't make that mistake in a relationship again.'

Every little difference will make you feel inspired and amazingly happier with yourself. Every day you're building your self-esteem a little higher so you're much less likely to put up with relationships that don't support you, and be attracted to more loving partners in the future.

CHAPTER 13

Dealing with Down Times

If my energy's good I'm fine. The worst thing is when my energy isn't good. I start thinking, is this my lot forever? And you can feel very victimy and 'poor me' about it. If I'm feeling depressed anyway and in a bad state, I think about being single and think is this it then? And why me? Is it too late now because I'm the age I am and everyone else is fixed up? There have been whole years when I simply haven't met anyone. There's been no one decent around. Men friends apologize for the state of other men folk in general. They say I understand why you're single, when we're such a rotten lot. I look around and agree. And think why bother? I've never felt wanted, just someone there. I have sometimes wished I had lesbian tendencies because women are a lot more interesting, but I don't. Often at times like that I realize I'm premenstrual or there's some specific reason for being down and it doesn't last.

Louise, a long-term single

When it's difficult is sometimes when I'm lying in bed. I think, here I am again. Bugger this. It's when I've minded most, lying there. I think boo hoo. A little plaintive thought will go through my head. Or when handling something like a difficult patch in life I'll think I'm tired of tackling this one on my own.

Maria

There are times when I feel tired or not well and just want to snuggle up on the sofa and watch a film with someone and have it be easy. There's quite a lot of effort involved in making contact with people when you're single. I also miss the sexual side, physical intimacy. The desire fades a bit, and that makes me feel a bit sad in a way – it does go to sleep.

Rachel

I remember a time when a fling I'd had with an Irish guy had ended and I used to just come home and think, 'I don't want to do anything. I just want to sit here and veg out'. I didn't like it. But I didn't want to do anything else either. I would resist calling him and I just had to stay with feeling miserable and lonely. And that kind of loneliness is the worst thing. Right now I'm OK with being on my own, but it's very up and down. The other day in Sainsbury's this woman was screaming, there was a man lying on the floor, and it really upset me seeing her crying and being comforted. I thought 'God, if I was here on my own, who would know I'd collapsed?' That whole thing about getting older and getting ill, that's the really scary bit. And I don't want to do that on my own.

Lynsey

You can be cruising along just fine. You can be thinking, this is all right, actually. And then, suddenly, boom, down you go. You get into bed alone yet again and soak the pillow because the yearning for some warm body (which isn't the cat) is just overwhelming.

It may be triggered by a specific incident. Such as bumping into your ex when you've got a cold and he's got a suntan. Or a friend gets married. Or your gran says: 'Still not met anyone yet, dearie?' Or the weather changes to how it was the time of year he left and some ancient part of your brain throws up memories of how awful it all was. Or you get ill or have problems at work and the thought of having to deal with it on your own brings the desperation on down.

I thought I was doing all right, five months after a break-up. I was busy at work, going out a lot, I thought the worst was over. Until the date of a friend's wedding loomed. I woke up that day feeling terrible, and cried for hours. I thought I was never going to get myself into a fit state to go, but I was helping her dress so I had to. She was marrying a wonderful, reliable, funny man who so adored the ground she walked on that if he could, he'd have bought the streets.

Great as it was, and pleased as I was for her, the whole day felt like a series of knives to the heart – seeing everyone so happy and smiling, seeing her husband so happy and handsome, seeing her so radiant and adored. Somehow I got through it, went home and cried some more. Until, after a few days of weeping, the feeling left as suddenly as it had descended.

You may – probably will – get down times that last a few hours, a few days, a few weeks. In Jane's case, it lasted a year. She says:

I was made redundant and I cocooned myself for a whole year. Just sat in my flat, listening to the radio and taping songs I liked and editing them down to make tapes I liked. And it was something I needed to do.

I realized a big fear of mine was being abandoned and actually being alone I realized how programmed I'd been into thinking this was a failure. That I'd fallen off the social plateau in some way. I decided to face it, rather than carry on with what avoiding it was making me do, which was going out just to have some sort of social interaction whether it was rewarding or not. And I brought that energy back in instead of scattering it over various pubs in the area. Eventually my life became redirected to what is now, a million times better.

A year was what Jane needed. (But don't panic and think that when the down times descend they may not lift for 12 months.)

They may only be moments. Like Louise in Chapter 10, I often have a wobbly moment when I see pregnant women or women with babies and think someone loved her enough to have babies with her. Babies are a symbol of ultimate commitment. My friend Laura says: 'I have times of sitting in front of the TV thinking, my life is over, I'm a washed up old hack and nobody loves me. But then I pull myself together, go out, have a flirt and feel a whole lot better.'

Down times are usually just another dollop of grief surfacing and, as my grandmother would say, better out than in.

And, lurking behind a down moment, is often some fear.

Jacqui grappled for many weeks with the 'What If I Never Find Anyone' panics. 'I felt so terrified about whether I'd missed my chance to have children at one point that I'd see spring lambs and burst into tears. I think all the fears and worries need to live in your head for a while while you subconsciously work them out. I don't know when my nervousness about not having children, or never finding anyone, began to go away. You just have to live with it. And then I found that it just worked itself through and one day I just wasn't so bothered.'

Sometimes down times come when you're just plain fed up with being on your own. As Louise puts it: 'When I'm fed up I have periods of what I call "resourcefulness fatigue". Yes, I *know* I'm resourceful. I do all the stuff around the house – putting shelves up and all that. I even go round to old boyfriends and put their shelves up, for God's sake. But I get fed up of being resourceful and think, can't I stop being resourceful for a bit and just collapse and have someone take care of me?'

Tips:

Be gentle with yourself. You will probably need extra nurturing during down times – and, ironically, it's the very time it tends to slip.

Tell someone how you're feeling. Do some emotional planning. Make sure you're not alone on hot days like anniversaries, Christmas, Valentine's Day. That means planning support.

Ditto, if you live alone, make sure you're doing plenty at times like bank holidays and Easter. Human beings are not meant to live in isolation and isolating yourself only makes you feel worse.

Remember down days are inevitable – it doesn't mean you're plunging into an endless depression.

Notice whether how you're talking to yourself is making things worse. If it is, go back to Chapter 4.

Avoid catastrophizing. It's usually fear or grief. Investigate the fear behind the grief.

Use your affirmations, and keep thinking positively.

Get some touch. A massage. Or ask a friend to give you a hug.

Is It Love? Or Is It Longing?

Sometimes single women can be assailed by periods of an indefinable yearning. It's easy to believe, if only I had a man this feeling would go away. Or if only I had the life I had with Fred back, this feeling would go away.

But perhaps it wouldn't. Perhaps what you're feeling is not love for Fred, but longing. Longing for something different, something you can't have. Which is understandable during the down times when being single feels plain miserable. We long for something to take the pain away. But often it's staying with the pain that makes the pain go away.

I've been assailed by longing at various times and it's very, very strong. I remember when I finally got the job I'd been striving toward for years. Part of me was ecstatic, yet I would walk to work each morning thinking: Why then am I still not satisfied? Why do I have this tight feeling in my chest? This sinking feeling in my stomach? I was hugely relieved when Bob Geldof brought out his book *Is this it?* I thought, there he is: fame, worldwide adulation, saint Bobhood, and he still isn't satisfied either. Thank God. It's not just me then.

Nowadays I've come to know and recognize it for what it is – longing for something I don't have. Longing for something magical to come along and make my life all right. Which can feel like love. Or like nostalgia. Or the feeling you get at the end of a weepy movie.

The very essence of longing is its indefinable quality. It can feel like longing for a lost love, or a love we never seem to find, or the blissful irresponsibility of childhood. It can take the form of a sense we're not quite in the right life, not quite achieving our life's purpose. It can take the form, as one dedicated yearner experiences it, of longing for a certain kind of weather. Even the dictionary has trouble defining longing. 'Yearning desire', says the Oxford English. Then, under yearning, it simply states: 'to long for'.

Leah has become an expert on longing via a series of disastrous relationships. She says

From the minute I started falling seriously in love, I started falling in love with emotionally unavailable men. Then I would have this icon to adore because he symbolized everything I wanted in my life and couldn't have because he was never there for me – he was off being unfaithful or drunk or whatever. So what I thought of as love was actually longing. And, of course, when I split up with them I got to feel it even stronger.'

Eventually, she came to realize what lay at the root of her longing:

I was *very, very close to my father as a child. He was like my best friend, brother, constant companion. I loved him hugely. Then he disappeared when I was 11. And I started longing for him. Missing him in a deep craving inside. So when I kept falling in love with unavailable men it was like I was setting myself up to feel the longing because that, in a bizarre way, was like having a connection to my father. That longing was what I came to identify with him.*

Meanwhile, Joanne was experiencing longing as an intense nostalgia 'for nothing in particular'. She says:

I felt it particularly in my teens and early twenties. It felt like an emptiness in the pit of my stomach, a kind of sadness and 'wanting'. I wanted a career, an exciting life, but I was also sometimes assailed by shyness and insecurity and fear. Nostalgia gripped me most then. I'd feel I wanted to run back to an earlier age in time – a historical period I'd seen in films which looked much less complicated than 20th century adult womanhood with all the choices and freedoms on one hand but terrifying demands on the other.

I don't believe the three of us are freakish saddos. We're all successful working women living effective lives in the world. And whenever I talk of longing it strikes a chord, particularly with women. Is it a perverse aspect of the human – or female – condition to be always wanting something we cannot have?

Lynda Field is a psychotherapist and author who has looked into longing. And she thinks women are 'seduced' by the state more than men. She says: 'Say the word longing and I think of a female languishing on a chaise lounge just waiting for a man to come along and bring the solution. And I do believe women do "longing" more. In any situation which knocks us off centre we will always go inwards looking for emotions and where we went wrong, which only feeds it.'

Lynda's theory on longing explains why, when we get (or don't get) whatever it is we wanted, there's always more longing to come. She says: 'Our biggest, deepest longing is actually for what psychologists call "self-realization". To become complete, whole. And that operates on three levels: body, mind and soul. If you like, it's like we're on this path toward our soul food destination, and we go off and eat junk food along the way. We go off via our addictions – to relationships we know really won't work, to our career, to substances that aren't good for us, pursuing excitement and adrenalin. You're really going after the big nourishment: to be at ease with yourself and your world, but every now and again you zip off and have a snack. But it doesn't fill the big longing inside, hence the feeling keeps on.'

Plus her theory explains why, if you are fixating, say, that if only you were slimmer the longing, the dissatisfaction with your life would disappear, when you lose the ten pounds you still aren't happy. As Lynda points out: 'You can become singleminded and just satisfy the need on one level, like the physical, which dieting would be. But you need to do all three levels. I've had three babies and that doesn't do it either. But all these things that make you feel better about yourself fulfill a part of the longing. They can be a package that helps you become more rounded as long as you are looking for things that satisfy body, mind and soul.'

Many of us have had childhood experiences of neglect, disruption, abandonment, that leave us with the sense of a hole inside that needs to be filled – like Leah's above, caused by her father leaving. Learning to fulfill our own inner needs does seem to plug the longing so its pull lessens as the years go by.

For myself, my longing has ebbed considerably now I work at a job I enjoy and feel completely fulfilled by – something the 'job of my dreams' never did. Leah has lulled her longing by becoming more aware of her patterns with men and slowly changing them to choose men who don't remind her of daddy.

And Joanne, who yearned for another age, has lost her longing by growing up and living fully in this one. She says: 'I think now my nostalgia was about being torn between the security of childhood and fear of all the change and frightening stuff like responsibility and the need to earn my own living and meet a man and find a flat and a job and all the scary stuff of adulthood. I feel it much less now because I have more of the things I want in life and I've done some of the things, like meeting famous people, I wanted to do and found them rather less thrilling than they're cracked up to be.'

Not that all three of us don't get assailed by inchoate yearnings every now and again. But I, for one, am less attached to the feeling and it passes more quickly. Similarly, Leah says: 'This summer I was on holiday and my boyfriend came and visited me for a while. When he got on the ferry to go back and I waved goodbye to him, I just felt a flood of the longing come. But at least now I understand

and I can think oh, here's the longing again. There's a bit outside of me which can see what I'm doing.'

Lynda Field agrees that the key to coming to terms with longing is that when we feel an attack coming on, we detach. She says: 'Sometimes, to be honest, it can be a gas to have longing for a little while. Go and have a longing experience – go out with someone unsuitable, fill up on that junk food. Do it, but be conscious. Step out of it and witness yourself and it's much easier to flick it off. When we go off on tangents it's usually about not being conscious of what we're doing. But if you're aware of what you're doing and you know you're going for a while into that black forest of longing, then you'll find your way back really easily.'

When you detach a little from longing, you're in control of it, rather than it controlling you. You can see it for what it is – an old friend who comes to tell you there are still goals to be achieved, needs to be addressed. So while the longing may not entirely go away, it can be an occasional visitor it's poignantly pleasant to spend time with, rather than a live-in lodger who drains all your energy and kicks up too much racket in the hall.

CHAPTER 14

Forget My Feelings, What if the Car Breaks Down?

'I decided I had to learn to be the man. I was broke after my boyfriend left so I had to find the cheapest plumber, the cheapest locksmith. Then my car decided to go fall to pieces on me and I had to buy a car, all by myself, and get the best possible deal I could. I ended up with a purple Fiat Panda, and it gives me a great thrill every time I get in it, that I chose and bought it myself. I had to bite the bullet about feeling scared and wimpy about these things.'

Leah, on one of the more irritating aspects of being single

Being single isn't just about dealing with the ticking of the biological clock when there's no biology happening. It's also about being home alone when the light fuse blows and you forget where the fuse box is. Hell, what is a fuse anyway?

The world is made up of two types of people, whatever their gender. Those who cope admirably and practically with all life's doing words, and those who wouldn't know how to hang a picture, let alone a shelf. If you tend toward the latter of these two extremes, here's the guide for you.

The phrase 'I can't do it' leaves you terribly powerless. You can, actually. And once you start learning to take these things into your own hands it's immensely satisfying.

Won't Car Mechanics Rip Me Off?

- Motoring organizations such as the RAC and AA run 'approved garage' schemes for members and should be able to recommend a local one. (It's a good idea to join one of these anyway – if your car breaks down you can avoid 'helpless woman' status by calling one of these on your mobile).
- Write down any noises or problems before you go. Don't try to be technical – just describe them.
- Ask lots of questions. Ask the mechanic to be specific about the repairs and to write down an outline of them.
- Get quotations from several garages and make sure they include VAT, parts and labour. If the quote is written, then the garage is legally bound to do the work for that price (a verbal quotation isn't binding).
- If you can afford it, go to an officially franchised garage for your marque of car. Because their work is authorised by the manufacturers they have to provide a high

standard. My Rover garage is run by a woman, which helps my confidence about them.

- Remember – go in with the attitude you're the client and they're there to service you, as it were.
- If it's your first time and you're really not confident, get one of your new male friends to come with you.

Isn't It Dangerous To Live Alone?

Not if your home is secure. And anyway the average burglary happens between 2pm and 4pm when most of us are at work. However, you don't want to be taking any risks…

- Avoid buying or renting a ground floor or basement flat as these are more vulnerable.
- Make sure you have good locks on all the doors and windows. Your home contents insurance probably requires this anyway.
- More than 60 per cent of homes don't have window locks and most burglars come in through the window.
- Make sure you have good quality locks on the doors. These should have only one combination and extra keys can only be cut by showing identification at authorized locksmiths.
- Only lend your front door keys to people you really trust.

- Install automatic security lights – sensor-operated floodlights which come on when anyone approaches the house.
- Make friends with your neighbours so they know when you're out or away.
- Your local police station can arrange for a crime prevention officer to visit and advise you on security for free.
- Ask a male friend to record your answerphone message. At least, never leave a message that tells the world you'll be away for the next two weeks.
- Stop newspapers and milk deliveries when you go away, and get a friend to pick up mail to avoid that telltale pile on the doorstep.
- Get those light timers that turn the lights on when you're out. Leave the radio or TV on when out so the noise makes it sound like someone's at home.
- A phone near your bed is reassuring. (As is a hammer under it!)

What Happens If The Lights Fuse?

Or the roof leaks? Or the boiler breaks down? Or the doors fall off? Yes, household crises are annoying, but you can handle them.

- Call the relevant trade association for a list of reputable firms in your area. If you want to check if a supplier is on their list or not, most associations will tell you over the phone.
- Gas – CORGI (01256 372200).
- Electricity – The National Council for Electrical Installation Contracting (NICEIC) (020 7564 2323).
- Building Work – The National Federation of Builders (020 7608 5150); the Federation of Master Builders (020 7242 7583).
- Ask friends and neighbours to recommend plumbers, builders, electricians and so on.
- Insist on a schedule of works before they start the job, no matter how small it is. This is to establish how long it will take, the materials needed and the cost of labour for each task.
- Never hand over money up front – pay the bill in stages and use any retained payment as leverage to make sure any problems are put right.
- Don't agree to a daily rate – it encourages them to spin the job out. Agree to a fee for the whole job.
- If you're not happy with the work, go back to the firm in question. Produce all the paperwork, talk through the problem methodically.
- If this fails, call the relevant trade association – many have a conciliation service you can use.
- If they don't you can take the contractor to the small claims court (for any amount under £3000). Often, the

knowledge you're serious will be enough to magically resolve things. Your local Citizen's Advice Bureau will help with the legal process.

What If My Finances Get In A Muddle?

Now most of us earn our own money we're more adept at handling it. Nonetheless, women worry more about not being able to handle their finances than men do; yet are five times less likely to go bankrupt.

- Financial advisors make their living from helping people get the most from their money – ask friends for a recommendation or look in the Yellow Pages to find one. An independent advisor (who's not obliged to plug one particular company's products) is best. Ask your advisor about his/her training, qualifications, how long they've been in the business and how many clients they have.
- Talk to three or four advisors and compare quotes and advice – if what they tell you differs widely, ask why.
- Make an appointment with your bank manager. Most banks have a personal banker these days. Talk to them before you get in a mess and they'll be more sympathetic if you do.

- Keep asking questions until you really understand. It's your money.
- You might like to investigate a career development loan. There are often more financial options available than we realize. And if you don't know about them, you can't take advantage of them.
- On the subject of finances, make sure you've got a pension. Young women are woefully bad at getting themselves sorted with this kind of thing.
- Read the financial pages of newspapers like the *Daily Mail* which are geared to simplifying things for non-numericals.

What If I Can't Afford It?

We're so often told two can live cheaper than one that we tend to panic when one moves out. Recent research has proved this to be a myth. Part of the reason for this myth is couples spend more time at home whereas singles are buying their singles in a bar, not an off-licence. But there are savings:

- Many firms offer cheaper car insurance for women drivers who don't have any named male drivers on their policy (because women have fewer accidents and make fewer claims).

- Home insurance premiums are cheaper when you own half as much stuff given insurance premiums are calculated on the volume of your possessions.

Am I Safe On The Streets Alone?

Government statistics reveal that men are actually more likely to be mugged than women. A man aged 16 to 29 is four times more likely than a woman to be attacked by a stranger. For a woman aged 30, the risk of suffering a random attack is just 0.5 per cent. Nonetheless, you don't want to be taking any chances.

- Don't be afraid to seem rude or paranoid by nipping into a pub if you think you're being followed.
- Trust your gut instincts. Women who are attacked usually report 'something' told them they were being followed.
- A female friend, or group of them, is just as much protection as a man.
- Avoid deserted subways, dark alleys and short cuts after dark, even if you are with a man.
- 'Car jackers' are opportunistic – they don't lie in wait for you. Driving with your doors locked and windows and sunroof closed will keep you completely safe.

- Join the RAC or the AA. They give priority to lone women who break down.
- Buy a mobile phone – you can call for help from the safety of your (locked) car.

25 rules to be single by

1. You do not date any crappy man, just because he's better than no crappy man.
2. You do not do anything you really don't want to do.
3. You do not attend a party when you're ill and exhausted 'because *he* might be there' or 'because *the one* might be there'.
4. You do not scare yourself with the 'what if I never meet anyone' thought.
5. When you feel low, you ask for help and support.
6. You do not criticize yourself for past mistakes.
7. You do not obsess about how wonderful your ex was. Or how awful your ex was.
8. Other women's men are off-limits, even if it's them doing the chasing.
9. You say no to people who demand your time, energy and attention and never give anything back.
10. You are capable of doing your own drilling, decorating, door-painting. Or of paying someone who can.

11 You look after yourself, which means eating well and regularly, and nurturing yourself when necessary.
12 You keep yourself safe, including practising safe sex and not doing anything physically endangering.
13 You know for sure that a man, once a liar, cheat, thief or woman-beater, is always a liar, cheat, thief or woman-beater.
14 You accept shit happens in life, love and friendships and when it does you get over it and move on.
15 Your feelings matter.
16 You matter.
17 You know you can make your own decisions and live with the consequences.
18 You can support yourself financially without a man.
19 You can spend a Saturday night in on your own without chewing the curtains.
20 You don't let your parents treat you like a little kid again, now you're alone again.
21 You enjoy your own company.
22 You do not feel guilty or obliged when your friends fix you up with godawful men.
23 The words 'I'm no good with men/relationships' never pass your lips.
24 You do not indulge in man-bashing, however tempting to do so.
25 There are no rules. If you really want sex on a first date, do it.

CHAPTER 15

Sex and the Single Girl

I'd gone out with someone most of my life until Richard and I split up when I was 33. And I'd never really been into masturbating at all, partly because I always had a boyfriend there. After I split up with Richard, a magazine launched which was like Playgirl for women, and as I was working in magazines at the time, I bought it. In the back were loads of ads for dildos. I sent off for a big brown package full of them with my Barclaycard, and had the most fantastic fun time with my own body. I got a huge buzz (bad pun!) out of the pack arriving. I only ordered things that were really cheap and made in Hong Kong and the sex toys all fell to bits virtually the minute I used them. But that was part of the fun. And it didn't feel dirty or seedy, it felt like a celebration. There was no element of sad bastard with no one to have sex with. It was like, Oh goody I've got time and space to enjoy myself.

It was hot summer, the bedroom windows were all open and I enjoyed it a lot. So much so that when they'd all bust I went out and bought myself a proper vibrator for keeps.

Now I really like sex with my boyfriend and I really like sex with myself and they're two very different things. If I'm honest I wouldn't say one is particularly better than the other, just different and I get something very different from both of them.

Leah, on the delights of a sexual relationship with yourself

Just as it's hard to love anyone else if you don't love yourself, it's nigh-on impossible to have a successful sexual relationship with anyone unless you know your own body. In order to educate anyone else as to what you like in bed, you have to know your own body's secret pleasures – what turns you on, what you like, what you don't like, what induces bliss, what hits the bullseye and what misses the mark.

Now is an excellent time to practise. And meanwhile, you are utilizing the sexual law of use it or lose it. All of the long-term single women I spoke to said desire gradually ebbs away as single time goes by.

As Jane, seven years single, puts it: 'I do miss the sexual side. I miss the physical intimacy and I think desire fades a bit, that side of you does go to sleep, compared with how I feel when I've just broken up with someone. That makes me feel a bit sad in a way. And there's an element in the way I behave that would be different. I'd dress differently in a relationship, sexier, more attractively. I get more pleasure in dressing for somebody else. I would wear different sorts of clothes. You can get pretty lazy about the way you dress and it would be nice to have a reason to put more effort in, but there's just not the motivation.'

Of course, while you're single, you don't only have to have solitary sex. Some women have the best sex of their lives while officially without a partner. Now all those old rules about sleeping around making you a slut have all but disappeared, freedom can offer the time and opportunity to experiment with your sexual self. Many women report feeling freer on flings or one-night stands to try things they'd worry about trying with long-term boyfriends.

Like Ella, who says: 'While I was single I never went without sex for more than four weeks.'

Or Joanne:

I met this guy at a wedding and I didn't particularly fancy him. He called up and I was thinking what's the point, it's not going to go anywhere, and the other part of me was thinking, it's a night out, why not just enjoy it? Those two thoughts are always in my head. So I went, and though my relationship with him was short, it was the sexiest relationship of my entire life. It just felt good in my body even though my head was saying this is crazy, you have nothing in common, he's got naff tastes, he's got the most awful ideas about a lot of things, you disagree all the time. But we didn't get out of bed. It was just so passionate. And we tried all kinds of things I'd never done before, because *I didn't want a big relationship with him, I felt I could be any way I wanted. I always felt like I was a baby – how a baby would respond to just feeling without all that head stuff getting in the way.*

You can get profound gifts from short flings with men you'd never want to stare at across the dinner table on a regular basis. (Remember the barrier bonk in part one?)

Joanne adds:

I was married for 22 years, but it was never a very sexual relationship. And I met him really young. So when I split a year ago I had a lot of catching up to do. And the first guy I slept with was just wonderful in bed. It made me feel quite sad that I'd put up with so little for so long. But also it restored my faith in myself sexually. I was beginning to think maybe I couldn't get turned on. So now great sex is a vital aspect for me because that's the bit that was missing with my husband. So it's raised my standards for my next long-term relationship. I want lots of great sex.

A little flirtation does wonder for the ego, reinforces the fact you're a beautiful, desirable woman. Yes, I know I've said a lot about how we need to know this for ourselves, but the excitement of getting it from someone else never pales.

And whatever you're doing, you won't be alone. Statistics vary wildly – *The National Survey of Sexual Attitudes and Lifestyles* (Penguin) found over half of women aged 25 to 34 had had no sex in the previous four weeks. Whereas a survey for *FHM* magazine found single women reported having sex at least once a fortnight; and the most recent *Cosmopolitan* survey revealed 16% of single women have sex once a month. Some women take a decidedly forthright approach to the whole thing. Like Maria, who confesses:

If I was seeing someone I would sleep with them on the first or second night. There is no point in building up all the palaver if then they have a small willy, or they ejaculate prematurely or it's just all too much effort. Frankly I'd rather find out at the beginning than mess about and shilly shally and be let down at the end. I've only slept with ten men and half of them have been bad in bed. That's 50 per cent of men. They were all lovely men, but no use in bed. I like all that flirting, kissing, messing about, but if I do want to sleep with them, I want to sleep with them soon.

I'll say it again, *there are no rules*. Whatever works for you while you're single is fine. Just as long as you're enjoying yourself. And, obviously, practising safe sex and looking after yourself.

If you haven't already, now is a time when you could...

Buy a vibrator
Read a rude magazine
Dress as sexily – or not – as *you* wish
Buy an erotic book
Rent a soft porn film
Go on a girl's night to see the Chippendales
Buy a sex guide, or the *Joy of Sex*, and teach yourself to make love to yourself lovingly and expertly. Or read up on

what to do when you do have someone to do it with.
Rent *The Full Monty*
Explore a sex shop
Explore being gay
Buy sexy underwear – just for you

Exercise

Remember the romantic date with yourself exercise in Chapter 8?

Do it again but this time have a sexual date with yourself. Set aside an evening to make love to yourself. Obviously you need to give yourself the space, privacy and time you need. Have a long bath, give yourself a loving, all-over massage, then get carried away with yourself. Really spend time being sensual with yourself.

If you enjoy it, do this at least once a month while you're single.

The Special Cases Of Singledom

When you've never been single...

From the age of nine until I was 35 I was never without a relationship, and it is a really interesting space to get into. But that one period – of two years – when there was nobody was crucial, if I hadn't done that I don't think I ever could have moved on. It was absolute hell. But it was central to my feeling more independent and better about myself and being able to attract a different, healthier, kind of relationship.

Rowena, 36, on never being single

Until recently, this had been my experience too. And, of course, there's nothing wrong with serial dating, as long as you have it in perspective. However, serial dating or serial monogamy can become a habit whereby you avoid the tricky business of being on your own and forming that crucial relationship with yourself. And that relationship with yourself, as virtually everything in this book points out, is necessary for self-esteem and successful, nurturing, supportive relationships.

If there's never been no one...

- Without beating yourself up, just ask yourself a few questions. How satisfactory have your relationships with partners been? If entirely satisfactory, then fine. But if not, you might seriously benefit from being on your own for a bit.

- Go back to the chapters on mapping your patterns and busting your beliefs and remind yourself why it's so necessary to have a man in your life. If the answer lies in neediness, wanting someone to fill a hole created in childhood that never got met – or in unhelpful beliefs like: 'I have to have a man to feel OK and any man is better than no man at all' – bear in mind that it would help you to become your own support system and form beliefs that support your single self. After all, as the cliché goes, we come into this world alone; we go out of it alone. You can only enrich your life by enriching your relationship with you.
- You may be stuck in an addictive pattern. It is possible to be addicted to people or relationships in the same way as you can be addicted to substances like alchohol or drugs. And all addictions take us away from ourselves and factors about our lives we don't want to face.
- You can get help with this. You could consider seeing a therapist or counsellor. Or there are countless organizations for relationship problems – Relate, co-dependants anonymous, SA (sexual addiction).
- If you do decide now is a time when you want to be single and you never really have, be extra gentle with yourself, knowing you are changing years-worth of behaviour. You may need to wean yourself off men, not splice yourself off them. And when you feel ready, you know you'll do it. Being single need not be black and white, either or, it can be a continuum.

When you've never had a relationship... (or, at least, not for ages)

I've tried everything. Blind dates, dating agencies, the Internet, pen pals. And I just can't find anyone who matches up to the ideal relationship I'd like to have. But I'm really happy in my life, I have great friends, a loving family, I love my job. And I think, if this is all there is, it's OK, actually. It could be a lot worse.

Anne, 37, on how life doesn't have to revolve around a man

I talked to several long-term single women for this book, and their common experience was that being single for years can bring on a variety of emotional states from frustration and desperation to bewildered sleepless nights questioning: Why me? What am I doing wrong? On the plus side, you can build a life purely for yourself which then becomes extra difficult to share with anyone else.

- Without beating yourself up, ask yourself whether any deep-seated fears – of men, of relating, of commitment – stand in your way. Is it that you find relationships too threatening? Is it that you never get asked? Is it that you're never in a position to be asked? That you never put yourself in a position to meet anyone?
- Go back to the chapters on mapping your patterns and busting your beliefs and remind yourself whether anything emerged that might block you from participating in a relationship. Unconscious blocks can be so

powerful they cause us to emit 'unavailable' or 'uninterested' messages, even if, consciously, we are available and interested. Look at your beliefs around men, your beliefs around yourself. Are you holding yourself back from experience, not allowing to throw yourself fully into things for fear you'll be rejected, or hurt, or dumped? Do you believe no one would ever want you? or is your distrust of men or other people too profound?

- Have you let go of an ex? It may be that you're still not ready for another relationship. Sometimes it can take years.
- Are you too idealistic? Too attached to fantasy so that no flesh and blood man will stack up?
- Do consider therapy or counselling to help shift any blocks. Or to just get support for your single self. After all, if your car breaks down, you go to a garage and get it fixed. If your ability to have relationships needs attention, why not get help? The therapeutic relationship is just that – a relationship. Where you can practise relating in a safe environment. You could join a therapy group as a way of starting to practise having relationships.

Are you satisified with the rest of your life? If you face the possibility you may never have a relationship, can you live with that? If you have a rich social life, a home you love, a job you enjoy, maybe, like Ria, you may think, 'This is as good as it gets, and it's pretty good, actually.'

Summary of part two

In order to have a love affair with yourself, you are…

- Dreaming up – and creating – a wonderful single life for yourself
- Making the most of it, doing things your couply friends can't do
- Consciously building a relationship with yourself
- Creating a support network of friends, a single posse and cultivating male friendships
- Mapping your patterns so you have a greater understanding of yourself
- Investigating hidden beliefs about love, men, relationships
- Consciously doing all you can to boost your self-esteem
- Learning tactics for dealing with the down times
- Handling the practicalities of a single life – like getting your car fixed
- Having some sexual fun with yourself!

PART 3

Men Again

At some point you'll have to dip your toe back into that piranha-infested pond called dating...
Here's how to swim – and survive!

CHAPTER 16

Getting Ready for Romance

People often focus on how scary it is to go on a date, completely forgetting that dating is brilliant fun. You get to go to places you might not go otherwise, you get someone trying to impress you, you get to dress up and make a big fuss of yourself, you get all your friends gagging to hear how it went, and, if you're wise, you'll ask him what he found attractive about you so you get lots of compliments and your ego gets a large, satisfying boost.

Emma, 26, dating enthusiast

The thought that gives everybody a sinking feeling when they become single goes something like: '*Oh no, now I've got to go through all THAT again*'. At some point you'll have to make a trip into the dating minefield.

And just as you're not the same woman you were the last time you were single, you're now a different person dusting off that pulling dress again.

You may be tougher, or more tender; older and wiser. You may not trust you know how to pick the right man. Or you may know exactly what you're looking for. You may be terrified of the whole thing, or more devil-may-care. You may have become more cynical, or more idealisitic. You may feel your last love was a benchmark, or a bullet to rebound from.

You may be thinking: 'Right, now for the big one. The next one *has* to be right'. Or you may be thinking, 'I don't care who the hell I date now, given what's gone wrong in the past'.

But, hopefully, by working with the exercises in parts one and two and enriching your relationship with yourself you will now be much, much more confident than ever before.

Bear in mind that the first step to meeting Mr Right is to be thoroughly sick of Mr Wrong – *for you*. Remember what we've said about unhealthy patterns, unhelpful beliefs and lovemaps in parts one and two. You need to have a few workouts to build your relationship muscle, and kiss a few frogs before you can even begin to recognize anything remotely prince-like.

The women I talked to fell along a spectrum in their attitudes to dating. Whereas Rachel felt the longer she was without a man the more idealistic she became and the more convinced she wasn't going to waste time with anyone who wasn't right, for Jacqui the longer she didn't date the more desperate she became. Anyone would do, just as long as it was a date! Then there are differences – and difficulties – according to the lifestage you're at. Like Louise's joke that men after divorce are like parking spaces – all the best ones are taken and the rest are disabled!

Don't Worry – Be Happy

Whatever your personal dating agenda, you are using your time being single to become your own expert on love, intimacy and commitment. See yourself as a student of relationships. You're learning all the time what works, what doesn't. Some dates may be disasters, but you still learn from them. Some may be delightful – then they never call. But with every date you notch up a little more that you can put down to experience, adding to the data bank that will help you recognize Mr Right. Time spent dating is never wasted – even if it's a waste of time you'll be better at spotting a time-waster.

One of my friends, Sandra Donaldson, honed her dating skills so precisely after a few months of attracting every available man in the Portsmouth basin, that by March her friends were calling her 'one-date Donaldson'.

It doesn't matter whichever place you are approaching dating from, even if the old man only moved out last week, the big question is: how do you deal with your new improved self on new possibly-not-improved dates?

There are a few guidelines that can help.

Did you skip the middle part and turn straight to this bit?
Fair enough. Just bear in mind, the thought: 'I have to find someone else' makes you desperate. That's why the whole process of being single and loving it does you good and prepares you for the dating circus.

A New Way to Find your Perfect Partner – Without Leaving The House!

Chance is always powerful. Let your hook be always cast; in the pool where you least expect it, there will be a fish.

Ovid. Not a single woman but a Latin poet born in 43BC.

How to attract the man of your dreams. Step one – dream!
Look at your life. It reflects what you desire on a very deep level. It reflects what you expect. The kind of men you're attracting reflect the kind of men you *want* to attract on some level.

If you expect to be treated like something the dog brought in, that's what you'll get. Until you get so thoroughly sick of it you're mad as hell and decide you're not going to take it anymore.

A surefire way you'll be able to recognize Mr Right when he comes along, is to be clear about what it is you want – from a man, from a relationship, from your lovelife, from life. What's right for you may not be right for everyone. And what's right for you now may have changed from what you thought was right in the past.

This may sound unromantic, but it's a competitive marketplace out there – the love jungle. And it's important to be as forearmed as possible.

It's a funny thing, but when you're clear about what you want, you stand more chance of getting it. It makes sense. If you're sceptical it can happen in love relationships – an area we tend to invest with all sorts of dreamy fairy story ideals – think about how it happens in your career.

You have to know what kind of job you want, or you won't even get on the first rung of the ladder. You don't just hang about in the job marketplace, hoping a job will wander over and buy you a drink. People often ask me how I got into the 'glamorous' world of women's magazines. Well, I had to *want* to first. Then I had to do something about it. Then luck came into play. But until I knew it was what I wanted to do, obviously I didn't get anywhere.

The reason for being clear about what you're looking for is it can speed the whole process along. If you think, for example, I'm sick of doing all the giving in my relationships, next time I want a really caring man; already a part of your romantic antennae will be on the alert for 'caring'. You will pick up more quickly on any signs of uncaring behaviour. You won't suddenly wake up three years into a relationship and think, Buggeration, he cares about the spiders in the bathroom more than he cares about me.

Madonna agrees with me on this; a woman who has wanted many things in her time – fame, a film career, a baby, a husband who beat her up – and got most of them. Blue-tacked to my computer is a quote I pulled out of a Madonna interview in *Vanity Fair*: 'When you want something bad enough the whole earth conspires to help you get it.' Ignoring the appalling grammar for a moment, it's true.

Not that Madonna discovered this universal principle by herself. Apart from world religions, which have called the practice 'prayer', the psychologist Carl Jung coined the phrase 'synchronicity' for the way life tends to throw up coincidences which spookily offer us what we've asked for or give us what we need. Or you could call it serendipity. Or pure luck.

But you can make your own luck.

This has probably happened in your own life. You decide you'd like to be a voice-over performer and you bump into someone at a party who is a voice-over agent. You decide you'd like to resuscitate your childhood love of singing and the next day you find out someone you know is in a local choir. You decide you need a holiday even though you're broke – and that week a colleague tells you of a brilliant new bucket-shop he's discovered. Even as I was writing this chapter, as if life was trying to prove a point, a friend gave me a book on astrology and I opened it on a chapter suggesting rituals for attracting your perfect partner which, as a vote of thanks, I've included below.

This kind of thing happens so often it has to be more than pure coincidence. It's coincidence working in our favour.

Once you get clear about what you'd like in your lovelife, coincidence starts working on it.

The way to get clear is get deeply practical and...

Make a List

My best friend did the list. She requested a man who was good-looking, interested in spirituality (as she was), an artist (as she was). She even required he have a 'fat willy'. She met him, of all places, by going to hear the Dalai Lama, the spiritual leader of Tibet, speak at Wembley. Hardly the most obvious pick-up joint. He was gorgeous, interesting, intelligent. He was an artist living in Cornwall. And, having met him where she did, obviously the spirituality issue was sorted. (And, yes, the willy thing was right too.)The only sticking point? He didn't have a job. She says: 'When I was making the list, I'd thought about whether I should say he had lots of money and I decided not to. And I just didn't think about what kind of job I'd like him to do. So what did I get? Someone with no job and no money at all.'

US author and relationship expert Barbara de Angelis believes in making the list, too, and suggests writing it out and carrying it around in your handbag. In her book, *Are You the One for Me?*, she says: 'I believe the list can actually act like a magnet, attracting that special person into your life.'

What you'll find, like magic (and it is magic) is you get what you ask for.

What to do:

Here's how can you get life's delivery service working in your favour on the love front...
Make a list of all the qualities/attributes you'd like your ideal man to have. Bearing in mind the following...

His physical style – is he a snazzy dresser? Slim or chunky?
Emotional style – is he caring? In touch with his emotions? Loving?
Social style – outgoing or appealingly shy?
Intellectual style – clever? Knowledgeable?
Sexual style – a demon in the sack? Or competent and not over-demanding?
Communication style – does he love to talk? About what?

Professional/financial style – does he enjoy his job? Financially solvent?
Personal growth style – is he self-aware? Does he take responsibility for his actions?
Spiritual style – is he religious?
Interests and hobbies – are they the same as yours? Or different?

Some pointers...

- When looking for men, we tend to over-focus on the physical. Don't obsess on physical attributes, unless there are some that, hand on heart, are an absolute necessity. Like if you're 5' 10" and won't go out with anyone shorter.

  You're not going to reject him if he doesn't have a hairy chest. *Are you*?

  As we know, your type may not actually *be* your type. Just because black-haired, moody males with crooked noses always make you weak at the knees, it doesn't necessarily mean they possess the qualities necessary for a long-term partner. (Apologies to all black-haired, moody men with crooked noses who are perfectly well-rounded human beings.)
- Be specific. Don't say 'nice'. Detail what nice means to you. Don't say 'good with children', it's too vague. Does he *want* children? Does he have them already so you don't have to have any? Adores yours? Or just likes being with children? Don't say 'reasonably intelligent'

or 'cleverer than me'. What does *that* mean? Say 'graduate', say 'brain surgeon' if that's what you want.

- Think about the qualities you want him to have, *and* the qualities of how you want him to behave towards you.
- It's fun to do the exercise with a friend. You get to share your wishes, hopes and dreams, and you can help one another get specific; tell one another what you've missed out. She might notice that you've left off, say, having interests in common.

For example:

Here's my list, created March 1999. Informed by past experience and current desires.

My ideal partner:

Intelligent

Funny – makes me laugh

Witty, articulate

Has an interesting job he loves

Is happy with himself and who he is

Is open-minded about all my weird beliefs

Can cope with me being a successful woman in the world

Supportive

Capable of love and commitment

Caring – and capable of behaving in a caring way without feeling he's giving himself away

Is his own person. Can be on his own

Doesn't take any shit from anyone (including me)

Has resolved his relationships with his parents
Can get angry and express it rather than storing it up and bearing a grudge
Is attractive in his own way
Can get on with my friends
Is not looking to me to make his life OK
Has a modicum of maturity. He can act like a little boy and be playful sometimes but being a little boy is not all he essentially is
Is interested in spirituality
Is sexually compatible with me. Can make love and look me in the eye at the same time
Is OK about my age
Is willing to change and grow from experience
Is solid and reliable
Doesn't mind about my need for independence. Lets me go off and do things without him and has things he likes to do without me too
Is financially solvent, isn't stingy and isn't interested in how much money I might have or what he can get from me in that department
Regards a relationship as a partnership. Is capable of sharing and wants to be part of a team – i.e. is not competitive with me and trying to get one up on me all the time
Thinks I am an amazing woman and he's lucky to be with me

Is capable of an intimate relationship – has a willingness to explore intimacy and not run away from it
Is a communicator who talks to me about what's going on for him in life and in our relationship. Doesn't withold because he's afraid
Is capable of trust and is trustworthy
Oh, I nearly forgot, has interests and activities in common with me…
(And just in case you are wondering – or need further proof that this method works – I found *exactly* this man)

A note of caution…

Be careful what you ask for, you just might get it. And you know the old saying – there's only one thing worse than not getting what you want and that's getting what you want.

You may get what you want in unlikely ways. Life has a habit of playing games with us. You might have asked for a man who's a company director, but are you prepared for the hours he'll have to put in with a job like that? You may never see him. You may be left alone looking after the kids. Or, if you've asked for a millionaire, will you be capable of handling the lifestyle he might provide? That will certainly challenge any self-esteem glitzes, any 'I don't deserve' beliefs that might still be lurking around.

Now you've done your list, some points to ponder…

Watch out for asking for opposite qualities to the ones you have. That indicates you're looking to someone else for compensation of your own weaker points. For example, if you've asked for someone who will be the life and soul of the party because you're not, just be aware your own self-confidence might need a little improvement. If you've asked for someone with lots of money, ask yourself what you're worth and whether you need to ask for a rise. Taking responsibility for what you're afraid of and doing something about it makes it come in quickly. This way, your list can be a tool for self-awareness (everything becomes a tool for self-awareness in the end).

Go down the list again and ask yourself: Do I have these qualities? I can't prove this by any kind of science, but, when it comes to love relationships, like really does attract like. I know it's true in my life. I see it in my friend's lives, and I read it anecdotally in all kinds of self-help literature.

Think about yourself in your life now. If you know deep down you're not really over your last relationship and are still carrying a caseload of anger around, think how you'll feel about attracting someone who's still not over their ex and is carrying a caseload of anger. If you can't be on your own, do you really want a man who can't be on his own? Because this is what you'll get. It's like some relationship law of precise returns – or, as Lou Reed put it in 'Perfect Day': 'you're going to reap just what you sow'. We get back what we put out.

So investigate your motivation very carefully and be honest with yourself. You needn't tell anyone about it.

When you've done your list:

You could increase the power of the whole process by doing a little personal ritual. Through the ages ritual has been used to invoke creativity, to focus intention and to call in a force greater than ourselves. It can't do you any harm. And it can be a lot of fun.

- A group of my friends often do the list on a full moon (when the moon, often seen as a powerful feminine force, is at its most powerful). Or a new moon (great for starting new things). We drink fizzy wine, go out into the garden and tell the moon what we want. Whatever you do, have fun doing it. Shout it out of your open window.
- Utilize a little Feng Shui, the ancient Chinese art of placement, and pin your list (or put it in a box or jar) in the creativity area of your home/room. This is the place of manifesting what you want. As you enter your home/room through the door, it is in the middle of the area/wall to your right. Alternatively, put it in the relationships area, which is the far right hand corner opposite your entrance.
- If you believe in God, pray for it.

- In homage to the spirit of synchronicity, here's the Venus ritual from Caroline Casey's *Making The Gods Work For You* (Piatkus):

  On a Friday, take a round piece of bread (like a roll), make a hole in it, put a 5p piece inside (the number 5 is sacred to Venus). On top of the coin, place a small piece of folded paper on which you have written your list. Put a little honey on top of that, for obvious symbolic reasons, then place a short yellow candle in the hole. Light the candle.

  You can do anything you want while the candle is burning. Honour Venus: play beautiful music; prepare your home for Venus's arrival. When the candle is completely burned down so that only melted wax remains on top of the bread, take it to sweet water. Go to a river or pond and throw the biodegradeable bread-candle remains into the water while saying: 'I am the presence bringing into my life my beloved, free and willing to be my mate and partner. I am so inspired that I find the courage to play and the wisdom to love with a cheerful heart.' This ritual always seems to work.

It sounds silly but, when it comes to love, I bet we've all done sillier.

Remember affirmations and create some affirmations around this, like 'I now attract my perfect partner into my life' or 'I am now attracting a loving, happy, committed relationship'.

Finally...

Do your list, do your ritual. Then forget about it. Don't keep obsessing about it. Try and cultivate a 'quietly confident' attitude. The US queen of visualization, Shakti Gawain, advocates consciously visualizing yourself having what you want, then leaving it up to fate to sort out the rest. She says: 'An important step is you have to see it, then let it go.'

And don't tell everyone. It's a secret between you and maybe the friend/s you did it with. Don't blab on obsessively about it at every dinner party over the next few months. This has a weird way of not letting it work.

Finally, finally...

If you do your list and you don't attract him as quickly as you'd like, ask if you have any blocks left. Any areas where you're not entirely convinced by all this. Because, believe me, when you believe, truly, deeply, madly, he comes.

(And if you attract any unsuitable lovers doing this exercise, don't blame me, blame cupid.)

CHAPTER 17

Dating Without Tears

If a man comes on to you, even if you're glad of the attention, for God's sake try and hide that. You should behave as though that's your due, which it is. For everyone. We all have something about us which can enchant, but if you behave like it's a huge compliment that someone's noticed it, you really are short-changing yourself.

Maria, hard line advocate of dating from a place of high self-esteem

The key to dating without tears is balance. Don't make it all-important, don't make it the only thing you do. Keep up with your women friends, don't drop them just because you're dating. You'll need them still for support and they won't be well pleased if you're the type who only calls when there isn't a man around.

When Joanne split up with her long-term partner she set about a full-scale manhunt. She spent hours every night chatting with men on the Internet, spent every weekend on blind dates. As she confessed 'I didn't bother with my women friends. I don't have a huge amount of girlfriends and I don't know anybody round where I live. So it's not like I'm out and about all the time. I do have a friend, but then I don't make the effort. So it's a vicious circle. I could go out with her. And I don't make the effort.' This was Joanne's choice as to how she runs her life, but if looking for a man is all you do you run the risk of becoming desperate and obsessive and unhappy with yourself.

So lighten up. Don't take it all deadly seriously. Dating, believe it or not, is supposed to be fun. Date more than one man and each becomes less important. If your life gets complicated, then stop it. Don't sleep with them just because they ask or to find out what they are like.

The world does not begin and end with this date. You're just meeting up with someone. You are not a contestant in the date olympics, competing to be the prettiest, wittiest, most perfect date ever (oh, and potential mother of his perfect children). Acting as though you are raises the stakes sky high.

You're just having a coffee with another human being who happens to be a man.

And someone finding you attractive can be a wonderful, thrilling affirmation. Just enjoy it.

Yes, dating can give you the most thrilling feelings of excitement and exhilaration when it goes right and the most appalling downers when it goes badly. The trick is to minimize the downer dates and up your chances of hitting a bullseye. Fortunately you have all the tools to do this right now. You just may have to go down the shed, and give some of them a good old polish.

Remember rule 25 of Rules to be Single By, when it comes to dating…

HERE IS THE RULE: THERE ARE NO RULES
You can date several men at once, date a man once and say goodbye, have sex or not have sex. It's up to you. You can make your life as simple or as complicated as you wish. If you meet a wonderful one, then another comes along, date him too. A date is not a contract. A kiss is not a promise. Even having sex does not necessarily *mean* anything. All it means is you wanted to have sex with one another.

The dating arena is an excellent place to practise new skills such as self-awareness, your knowing what you want and need and your courage in speaking up and stating it.

The advantage of becoming more clear and assertive is once you feel the thrill it gives you, once you realize the experience of how much easier it makes your life, you start using it all over the place. With your boss, with your mother, the man who comes to sell dusters at the door, whoever.

Like Therese, who says:

I married the first boy I ever went out with. So when we broke up ten years later, I felt I really didn't know how to date because I'd never done that teenage thing of dating then chucking them a week later and moving on to the next. I was terrified. But after I'd done it a few times, I realized this was a brilliant way of experimenting with my new self, of doing things differently. These people didn't know me, so I could be as upfront and assertive and demanding as I wanted. And, bizarrely, I found the more myself I was, the more the men seeemed to find me attractive. Within six months I was beating men off with a big stick.

Work that Flirting Muscle!

We all know someone who attracts men like flies, even when she's no Michelle Pfeiffer. I know a woman who will turn up at a club in a tracksuit top and chinos when all the other women look like they've dressed for the Oscars, and within minutes she'll be surrounded by men. It's something in the way she holds herself. The way she looks entirely comfortable with herself, even when dressed all 'wrong'. She looks relaxed, happy, approachable. The message she gives out is: I like myself. I bet you'd like me too.

It's called confidence.

What you can do to boost your confidence

- Make sure you look the best you possibly can. Get yourself a makeover. Get yourself a new haircut. Or a nosejob. Go to a shop and get them to tell you the clothes that look best on you. Treat yourself to a visit with an image consultant like Color Me Beautiful.

Looking the best you can is all part of loving yourself. You always feel more confident when you know you look good.

- Get your friends to tell you what your strong points are – and enhance them.
- Make some confidence-boosting affirmations. Look back on the work you did around your beliefs in chapter twelve. Tell yourself you're confident, sexy, intelligent, funny, witty, smart.
- Wear red. It's a bright, sexy, confident colour. Notice how you feel in different colours.
- Wear red lipstick.
- Get fit. Get your body looking the best it can. Dress so you enhance your body's good points.
- Relax. Be yourself. Be gorgeous.
- Start flirting!

Flirty moves

Flirting is an art which, like any art, improves with practice. Yes, certain natural assets are an advantage, but the fine thing is we all have them. Yes we do.

Here's what women do when they want to convey a certain amorous interest. When you're confident and interested you do this naturally. If you're shy and wish you weren't you may just have to learn how to send flirt signals.

Flirtation first came under the eyes of the scientists over 30 years ago when a Viennese researcher, Irenaus Eibl-Eibesfeldt, discovered that people in cultures all over the world, from the South Sea Islands to Southsea, signalled sexual interest in the same way. Women, from those who have no written language to those who regularly read *Cosmopolitan*, use nonverbal signals that are very alike. So, if you want to attract a man anywhere on the planet, here's how you do it.

According to Eibl-Eibesfeldt it's always the females who signal interest first. She smiles at a male, then arches her eyebrows to make her eyes wide, quickly lowers her lids and, tucking her chin down and slightly to the side, averts her gaze, followed within seconds by putting her hands to her mouth and giggling.

This is what else you do:

You toss your hair. Gently swing your hips. Giggle, gaze wide-eyed. Flick your tongue over your lips and stick your chest out. Sway your hips. Gaze at him like he's Pierce Brosnan with a sense of humour.

Of all these flirting tricks, the most alluring is gazing. Stare at him like he's the most interesting picture you've seen since *Titanic* and he should, at least on some subliminal level, get the message.

Make him laugh

The other thing you can do is give your sense of humour a polish. A straw poll of men questioned for this book said the ability to make them laugh was far more important than breast size. Hmmm. Anyway. Learn some jokes.

One of my friends has a humour habit that sends men weak at the knees. She'll say something outrageously flirtatious, sexy, upfront – like, to a rugby player, 'with thighs like that I bet you're amazing in bed' and then coyly backtrack with 'I can't believe I just said that'. It works every time.

Body language signs he's interested

So much for your side of the flirting equation. How can you tell, without him telling you, he's interested?

- Eye contact. He fixes you with a steely gaze and keeps it going for far longer than would, say, the postman.
- He strokes his neck. New research on flirting says that, in the presence of a woman a man finds attractive, he indulges in instinctive, universal mating behaviour that puts him on a level with a male peacock. He arches his back, stretches his pecs, imperceptively sways his pelvis in a tame Elvis impression, swaggers and laughs extra loudly.
- He makes grand gestures. He whips out his cigarette lighter with a flourish and flicks it on like he's auditioning for one of those old silent movies. He tugs his tie and chugs his chin toward the ceiling. What's happening is an ancient part of his brain is enacting an urban pantomime of the kind of stuff randy apes get up to in the jungle.

- His pupils enlarge. Apparently this happens so the eye can take in more of the beloved object. Bear in mind, though, it's hard to tell in a nightclub. It may be a sign he's taken too many 'E's and is off his head.
- He touches or strokes his glass, his hand, his neck. One giveaway of body language is our miniature gestures echo the larger gestures we'd like to make if we weren't so inhibited. Ergo he strokes his glass because he'd like to be stroking you.
- He touches you in conversation. As above, only he's getting a little braver.
- He mirrors your body language. You move forward, he moves forward; you cross your legs, he crosses his.

Once you're gazing into one another's eyes, you're away on that delightful game called flirting. But inevitably, once you start tossing your hair and swaying your hips about the place, you will attract some unwanted attention. Here's how to send it sweetly on its way...

Saying No Gracefully (Even When He's Nice)

I have friends who will go out with anyone because they can't turn anyone down, they are too flattered to say no. It doesn't say anything about you when some spotty, paunchy twit fancies you. There are ways of being approached by a man that are actually insulting.

Sarah, 23, hard line naysayer

So, a really nice guy gives you the chat. He's pleasant, he's keen, but he's wearing Hush Puppies. Or his halitosis would frighten your cats. Or you're not sure what it is but whatever it is he just isn't *you*.

He asks for your number. Are you gonna be nice? Or are you gonna be honest?

Just recall what happens when you say yes but you mean no. Every time the phone rings your stomach gets a little sinking feeling. It might be your mother. It might be your best friend. But, it might also be him. So you don't answer the phone and suddenly you're a prisoner in your own home. Or you do answer the phone and it's him and you find yourself saying, yes, all right and then *oh my God*! Or yes, all right, but not this week and somehow he never gets the message and you have visions of yourself at 70 with a zimmer frame picking up the handpiece and saying, sorry not this week...

Plus, maybe you have to avoid all your favourite haunts in case he's there.

Do you really want your social life to be this complicated?

There are ways of letting him down gently so he doesn't feel like Quasimodo and you don't feel a heel. All men agree they'd rather get a quick no than a fruitless run-around. But who wants to hear the blunt, God's honest truth – I don't find you attractive? You don't want to say it, he certainly doesn't want to hear it.

Some lines which have been tried and tested:

The no. 1 favourite – the little white lie:

Sorry, I've got a boyfriend/I live with someone/I'm married

My boyfriend wouldn't like it if I gave you my number/went out with you

If he knows you're single however…

Sorry, I've just split up with someone and I know I'm not ready to see anyone

You're lovely, but you're just not my type

You're lovely, but you're just like my brother and it would be like incest (!)

Sorry, I'm just too busy at the moment

Some dos…

- If he persists say, Why don't I take your number? You're saying you'll take it. You're not saying you'll *use* it.
- Body language. Try and look relaxed. Smile and make eye contact. Keep your voice calm and say something like 'Thanks. I'm flattered. But I'm very busy'. Don't speak too quickly and respond with a downward inflection on the word busy while maintaining eye contact.

- Keep it light. Smile, if you're a joker, make a joke. Humour always takes the tension out.

Don't...

- Overexplain. Recall the maxim: never apologize, never explain. Apologize if you want, but don't get caught up in 'My boss is making me work all hours and although I'd love to I'm really exhausted and... and...' It only prolongs the agony.
- I avoid 'can't' – it sounds passive and suggests you'd like to but cannot. Which gives him an opening to persuade you that you can really or you could later.

Remember:

You are not responsible for his feelings.

You have the right to say no.

You have the right to spend your time how you see fit.

You also have the right to change your mind. Everyone does, all the time. Call him back and say, sorry, but I've been thinking about it and I was wrong to say yes, I really don't want to see you, I'd really rather not meet up. Or if you can't get his number, turn up on the date and say you've changed your mind and you're going back home. The world will not end.

Otherwise you get his hopes up for nothing. Wouldn't *you* rather be let down gently than be given the run-around?

CHAPTER 18

What if it's You who wants Him? The Shy Woman's Guide to Making Man Contact

I never asked a man out until I was 30. Therefore I only went out with men who asked me. And a friend pointed out that I wasn't doing the picking. Also I thought, it's always been traditional that men ask us out, but nothing's traditional any more so why not give it a go? So I asked a guy out I had my eye on and we ended up going out for six months. These days I have no shame – I ask men out all the time – and they love it...

Rosa, on taking destiny into her own hands

It's a minefield, showing someone you find them attractive. A survey by Dateline found only 23 per cent of men and 37 per cent of women find it easy to approach strangers. And approaching someone you *know* can be even trickier.

Surfing the Internet on dating, I came across a book called *Baby, All Those Curves and Me With No Brakes: 500 New No-Fail Pick-Up Lines for Men And Women*. I don't know about you, but my likely reply to that opening gambit would be:

Baby, All That Chat and Me With No Ears. Here are a few ways of getting your message across without getting into trouble. Or, maybe getting into the best kind of trouble.

Ways of Approaching a Man

The best advice is, keep it simple. If you work with him, keep asking him questions about work until one day you ask if he'd like to discuss it all over a drink in the bar round the corner. (Or, if you can, e-mail asking him out for a drink. The written word spares your blushes.) If you spy him at the gym, ask how to use a piece of equipment. Ask a man in the video shop to recommend a funny film.

Kate mooned over a man at work from afar for ages until she decided to change tactics:

Every Monday I'd make a point of asking him what he did at the weekend. It never seemed to involve anything of the girlfriend variety, so one time, when he said he'd been to the movies I said, bold as you like, why don't we go to the movies? He went bright red and said I'd love that, I'll look in the paper and see what's on and we'll make a date. Turned out, he'd liked me for ages but was actually quite insecure and didn't think I'd ever be interested in him.

If you don't know him...

Cosmo tried some pick-up lines which they practised on men on the street, in bars, and so on. They went like this:

> 'Hey, Mark! Oh, I'm sorry – I thought you were someone else.'
>
> 'My brother's birthday is next week and he wants some new trainers. Can I ask you where you got yours?'
>
> 'I see you here a lot. Would you mind if I bought you a drink?'
>
> 'I know this seems forward, but my friend just bet me £5 I wouldn't have the nerve to introduce myself to you. My name is...'
>
> 'Do you know a good coffee shop round here? I'm gasping.'

These all, apparently, led to conversations and even exchanged phone numbers.

Finding out if he's available

Remember rule eight in 25 Rules to be Single By? Other women's men are off-limits, even if it's them doing the chasing. Here are the tips for digging at availability clues – and how to have fun with them:

- A wedding ring, third finger, left hand.
- A ring on any other finger: you could ask if it's a wedding ring and see what kind of reply you get. Then you can subtly follow it up with 'Are you attached'?

- Ask him where he lives, then 'Do you live with anyone?'
- Ask him what he did at the weekend. If he offers no leading clues, come out with it and say: 'Did you go with your girlfriend?'
- If all these are too subtle and you still haven't found out the crucial info, stare at the space just above a guy's right ear and say: 'So, are you seeing anyone?'

If all this quizzing doesn't give him the hint and get him asking you out, and you're determined to hook this particular fish, you'll just have to do it yourself.

How to Ask A Man Out So He'll Say Yes!

OK, maybe you've done all of the above and he's obviously terminally shy or hideously slow. Or maybe you glimpsed him once across a crowded room and won't see him again unless you engineer it. Or maybe last time you saw him you were with someone and now you're not and he won't know that.

So ask him out, already.

It's a new millennium. All those rules about the man has to do the asking are so last century. If you want something, go get it girl. He may be the love of your life.

On the phone:
Advantage: He can't see you blushing. Or your best friend giggling in the corner. You've also got an easy backout if he says no.
Disadvantage: You have to know his phone number. You might catch him at a bad moment.

Via e-mail
Advantage: He can't see you blushing, he can't hear the nervousness in your voice. If he says no, the two of you need never even mention it.
Disadvantage: Technological gremlins which sweep your message into a communication black hole; if he doesn't reply you still don't know where you stand.

In the flesh
Advantage: You get to smile, flirt, pout and indulge every alluring body language thing you know.
Disadvantage: It's harder if he says no.

Ask him along to a group thing
Like a party, a softball game.
Advantage: It's casual. There are other people there.
Disadvantage: He may not realize it's a date. He may not turn up. He may get off with your best friend.

One that can't lose, apparently:

The Bet Technique

This only works if you meet at a party, or at work or some other social situation and is obviously no use for Mr Across-a-Crowded-Room.

It works like this: pounce on a piece of trivia you and Mr Cute have bonded over in your conversation. Song lyrics, Italian football players, whatever – as long as it's provable. Then bring up a point of dispute and say: 'Loser takes winner out to dinner'. If he agrees, you're checking into Date Central. If he says, no way, you know he's not interested.

It's a win/win situation. No matter who loses, you still get to go out to dinner.

Tips:

- Just do it! Think, what the hell. Everyone likes to be asked out, it's immensely flattering. When he says yes, it can feel like the most exciting, self-affirming thing.
- Do say: 'I was thinking, would you like to get together for a drink?'
- Don't say Um, er, um, er...
- Try a little role play. Practise it first with your best friend. Fantasize about what he'll say and how you'll respond. Then at least you'll get a laugh out of it.

- If he says no, say something like 'Oh well, it was just a thought. Never mind'. Don't try and persuade him. What are you? A masochist?
- Be specific. Saying 'Would you like to go to a film sometime?' has a way of turning into sometime never. Saying 'Would you like to go see xxx with me on Friday?' is far more specific and far more likely to get results.

What if He's A Friend?

This is an extremely common, extremely tricky dating dilemma.

You've cultivated your male friendship as per Chapter 10, then you find yourself feeling more than ordinarily friendly. The question is, does he?

You're only going to find out if you say something. And if you say something, there are real risks. You may lose a valuable friendship, which has a high level of emotional investment. You risk rejection (after all, *he* hasn't said anything). And you risk the embarrassment factor of all your other friends finding out afterwards.

You need to weigh up whether it's worth it. Remembering that, after all, friendship is the basis of any love relationship worth having.

You need to ask yourself how serious you are, think about what signs you've had from him. And if you decide, all in all, it is worth it, set about using every weapon in your flirting arsenal. Apply everything you know about body language. Compliment him. Hint rather than coming straight out with it.

Mary had been friends with a work colleague, David, for a year when the office Christmas party rolled round. They were chatting as usual, then had a dance. A slow record came on, they moved towards one another – and that was that. She says: 'It was electric. He said, "Shall we leave?" And we did and we've been together ever since. But neither of us were conscious of liking each other in that way until they played Marvin Gaye.'

But if non-verbal communication doesn't work, you might choose to bite the bullet and say: 'Do you know I find you attractive?' If he says something like, 'Yes, but you're Elaine', then you know where you stand. If he says, 'Sorry, I don't see you in that way' you can say something like, 'Never mind, we can still be friends' and have a little sob into your pillow later. It is very grown-up to acknowledge a mutual attraction, even if you don't do anything about it.

And if he runs away and just can't cope with it, what kind of a friend was he anyway?

Then again, you might end up happy ever after. Good luck.

CHAPTER 19

Dating Blind – But Not Blindfolded

The Art of Dating Someone You've Never Met

I feel like the Queen of the blind date. I've dated people I've met through Time Out and through the Internet and I've also been to a singles bar. There you look at someone and maybe you like the look of them, maybe you don't. The Internet and Time Out is the other way around. You talk, then you look. Often you fall in love with a pretty face and you think, it doesn't matter if he has different tastes, he looks pretty horny. And in the end it does matter. But if you disagree on a lot of stuff on the phone or Internet, and you don't see their face, it could be a missed opportunity. I just think, what will be will be.

Joanne, indeed Queen of the Blind Date

I've been on so many blind dates I should get a free dog.

Wendy Leibman, comedienne

Maybe there's no one around you find attractive. Maybe you've run out of people you're attracted to. Maybe you aren't meeting the right people. Maybe you're sick of hanging around in bars or even pottery classes hoping Patrick Swayze will come along and help you with your clay wobble. When the going gets tough, the tough get proactive. And getting proactive can mean calling in romantic reinforcements.

These days any stigma there might once have been about dating via a third party has shrivelled. Membership of dating agencies is booming, local papers now carry lonely hearts ads, and thousands are going online every day, logging on to dating chatlines via a new dating arena that, a decade ago, didn't even exist.

The UK's leading dating agency, Dateline, put the boom in membership in recent years down to the fact people no longer have a job for life and have to move around more. Press officer Pam Bathe says: 'Society has changed an awful lot in the past two decades and that to some extent is down to what happened in the late 1980s when we had the stock market shakedown. Now people are far more itinerant. They have to go where the work is. People constantly find themselves in situations where they have to relocate, and they don't know anyone. They haven't friends in the immediate area. So the logical thing to do is turn to a dating agency.'

This and the fact women are no longer content to sit around waiting for Mr Right to come zooming to their door on a white charger, means more and more of us are taking the process of romance into our own hands.

Moreover, the dawning of a new millennium seemed to speed things up. Dateline reports that while January is always their peak time – there's nothing like being alone at

Christmas and New Year to focus the mind on pairing up for next Christmas – the millennium increased that impulse to fever pitch. During January 1999 Dateline's new members doubled from a normal January – that being double a normal month anyway – and didn't drop. By January 2000, at the time of going to press, Dateline were predicting new members would increase again by between 50 and 100 per cent.

And take it from me, using outside agencies DOES work.

I've lost count of the couples I know who met through the small ads in London's *Time Out* magazine. There's the pair who, after she answered his ad, fell in love at first glance by the Natwest cashpoint machine in Leicester Square and discovered she was pregnant – with triplets! – three months later. Ten years on, they're still together. There's the couple who discovered on first phone call they lived in the same street. Seven years on they're still in the same house.

Or the divorcee who, despairing of ever meeting anyone, joined Dateline hungry for romance. She'd never actually dated a romantic man and joked to her best friend she'd marry the first one who turned up with a dozen red roses.

She met a lovely man one day and arranged to meet him the next. It was pouring with rain, her umbrella was inside out and they were meeting in the one of the world's most unpromising locations, the PC World car park. But the weather was all forgotten because there he was with a dozen red roses. She says: 'I almost said "I do" on the spot.'

She did get to say 'Yes' when he proposed a few weeks later and from then on everything went like clockwork. Even though, in the wedding industry's terms, their's was a whirlwind hitch-up, everything they wanted was available – even the restaurant where they met for their first date was available for their reception. And she found her wedding dress by sticking a pin in the bridal section of the Yellow Pages, calling up and finding they had just what she wanted – in her size.

Which all goes to show that, yes, fate uses dating agencies too.

The best thing that can happen, then, is you meet the love of your life. The worst thing that can happen is you have a couple of boring coffees with men who wouldn't spark your gas hob, let alone your heart. Meanwhile the fact you're taking destiny into your own hands is a great cure for that old bugbear: *What if I never find anyone?*

Which is an important factor, especially if you've been single a long time. Like Louise who says:

I didn't have a particularly satisfying experience using a dating agency in that I didn't meet a long-term partner. But what it did make me feel was that I was being proactive. That felt very good, very positive. I knew perfectly well I might not happen upon the love of my life, but I felt good because I was creating opportunities. It didn't feel fine that I wouldn't have those opportunities.

It just increased the odds of meeting someone, but each individual meeting was just as awkward as it would be if we'd met some other way.

Some people are put off because they think taking a scientific approach, like having an agency match you via a computer, is unromantic. But, as Pam Bathe says: 'It can be incredibly romantic, meeting under the clock with a rose in your buttonhole.'

And although you may not meet The One through an agency or the Internet, you may meet new male friends – and maybe meet 'The One' through them.

Kate says: 'As a result of dating through the agency I met one guy who I went out with for a few months – and he introduced me to scuba diving, which I now *love*. And I met Martin who's a sweet friend, who I'm terribly pleased I'm not having a relationship relationship with. But he's now one of my best friends and I've learnt a lot about what makes men tick through knowing him.'

Even so, all sorts of worries can surface when you use an outside agency or the Internet – what if I do this and I still don't meet anyone?

But what if you don't do it and you still don't meet anyone?

Perhaps the most profound advantage of using a third party dating service is when you meet over that first capucchino you know you're both looking for the same thing: love. Not merely sex, or 'I'm not sure I want a relationship'. A lot of those silly games never even get started. Hopefully you don't waste time or emotion on someone who puts on a good front but, it turns out, isn't available. And even if you do, the way you've met makes the whole situation easier.

Here's a guide to getting the best out of dating services…

Dating Agencies

Advantages: They do a lot of the groundwork for you and screen out obvious no-nos. Plus anyone they fix you up with has bothered joining a dating agency too, thus demonstrating an above-average desire to find a life partner. If you pick an agency which has membership with the ABIA (Association of British Introduction Agencies) they are governed by a code of practice which requires they give clear upfront information about fee structure so there'll be no prevaricating about your charge or refunds, plus they'll have to provide some indication of the number of members they have in your local area.

Disadvantages: Can work out expensive. Dateline's standard fee is £150 for a year's membership fee, including your first list of contacts with up to six names. After that, they recommend members apply for a new list of contacts once a month at £5 each. And, obviously, if there's no one who matches your requirements or triggers your heart, that money is wasted. Also, some small local dating agencies are exceedingly dodgy. Anyone can set up an agency and there are precious little regulations. In 1993 a bankrupt man who set up his own agency was jailed for drugging and raping women who responded to his ads. It is advisable to stick with well known, reputable names and those with ABIA membership.

Some dos and don'ts when using a dating agency:
Do...
Keep a positive attitude. Pam Bathe says: 'Sometimes negativity can be a self-fulfilling prophecy. Those who do best out of Dateline are those who go with the punches, dust themselves off and start again with a bright outlook. And who also aren't too prescriptive about who they meet up with. They're content if they get 60 per cent of their ideal partner, rather than down to the last centimetre in height.'
Keep a sense of humour. Like Louise, who says:

Some of the experiences I had with the dating agency were quite funny. The funniest was when, because I work as an illustrator, they tried to pair me up with someone who had given up his high-flying career to be an artist. It was an obvious thing to do, but actually it really matters to me if someone is into something I don't respect art-wise. The guy insisted that, before we met, I should see his art because, he said, if you don't like it you probably won't like me. I saw it and I was appalled. It seemed to be very immature and his gods in art are people I loathe. It obviously wouldn't work. The agency didn't understand that but it was clear to us. I said to them, his work is really very immature and probably so is he. I couldn't possibly support him producing dross like that.

Keep trying. A woman using Dateline was a divorcee with three young children and was on a very tight budget. She'd call men on her list while at the office and leave a message inviting them to call her. One guy on the list didn't have an answerphone. She kept calling but he was always at work. Then, one day, she gave it one last try. It turned out there was a train strike and he happened to be at home. She married him. Be realistic. Just because the agency thinks you'll get on, it doesn't mean you will. Louise says: 'They fixed me up with another guy who was interested in art, but not an artist. He loved the idea of going out with an artist, but he had a very nine-to-five job and my freelance lifestyle appalled him. Even though it's the lifestyle of most artists. I never know where my next job is coming from and he couldn't have coped with it all.'
Arrange a short meeting for the first face-to-face. Coffee or a brief lunchtime drink. That way, as Pam Bathe says, you can suddenly remember the dry cleaning you have to pick up if it's not going well.

Don't...
Over emphasize the physical. Often women will demand a man six foot or over and refuse to even

chat with males of smaller stature. Pam Bathe believes the biggest mistake members make is in being over-prescriptive about looks. She says:

I have said to women who want tall men, if you met at a dinner party and you were getting on really well, you found him attractive, and he stands up and he's below six foot one, are you really saying you're not going to go out with him? And some women say, yes, that's right. And that's OK, we're a service. We're here to give people what they ask for. But at the end of the day, it's the person, not the looks, that count.

Expect them to find you a millionaire. According to Dateline, women do tend to seek a partner who is financially secure or who is on a similar salary level. But the agency won't match on salaries (otherwise there is a danger they could attract 'gold-diggers'). What they do advise is your placing a few restrictions on the education of the partners you request (i.e. exclude lower qualifications). According to Dateline this pretty well assures any well-heeled woman will find an equally well-heeled man.

Rush into meeting. Agencies advise members to have at least two or three, maybe up to six, conversations, letters or e-mails, before meeting up. They don't advise meeting on the strength of one phone call, no matter how well you get on during it.

Feel obliged to meet if you don't like the sound of them. Say: 'It's been nice talking to you, but I'm not sure we're right for one another and I don't want to waste your time'.

Assume they're available. Anecdotal evidence suggests many married men use agencies or the Internet to meet women. Just check.

'Lonely Hearts' Ads in Newspapers and Magazines

Advantages: It's local. Or it's targeted at a certain type of person (if you use *Private Eye* you're going to get a different type from, say, using the *Cosmopolitan/Esquire* link-up, Close Encounters). You have complete control over how you present yourself. It's cheaper than an agency – London listings magazine *Time Out*, for example, charges £1 per word, plus £7 for a box number. Their average ad receives 15 to 20 replies. Because you don't have all the palaver of joining an agency, anyone might reply – even someone who would never normally do this kind of thing, but whose interest was piqued by *your* ad.

It can work. *Time Out*'s Lonely Hearts pages have been going for nearly 30 years. In that time there have been several Lonely Hearts weddings, including three sisters who all met their other halves via its pages.

Disadvantages: You can't see a photograph. You have to go through all the letters yourself and you may get some right weirdies. There's always a chance no one may reply. The phonelines can be horribly expensive – one friend called the *Time Out* Talking Hearts line, got interested and ended up spending £43, not realizing it was £1 a minute.

The issue of safety is obviously not as strong as with an agency – although if something did go horribly wrong when you replied to someone else's ad, the publication would have their records should you want to make a complaint to the police.

Writing Your Own Ad

7 top tips

1 Focus on you, not them. If you write about you, you'll attract people who like the sound of you. If you focus on what you want from them, you might narrow it down too much and exclude some real sweethearts with qualities you might not have thought to ask for.

2 Show don't tell. For example, don't say 'I have a sense of humour'. Make them laugh instead. *Show* that you are an educated and intelligent person via interesting word choices, a clear structure, and unusual, creative descriptions.

3 Creativity will make your ad stand out from the crowd. A personal ad can take any form you like. A poem, or a joke job description. One internet ad consisted entirely of movie titles – one after the other

– chosen and arranged to describe the person placing the ad.

4 Show them what ***you*** would want to know. Make a list of the most important things that you would like to know about someone before responding to an ad. Chances are, other people would want to know the same about you. If you work, in what field? Have you ever been married before? Are you looking to make some new friends, or do you want to find that one special person to settle down with for a lifetime?

5 Age isn't everything, but... It is where a lot of people start. Do include your age in the ad. If you don't want to give it away exactly narrow the range: 'early twenties' or 'mid forties' for example. If you are 40 but feel 16, say so. If you are looking for someone outside your own age range, give a range for them as well. Bear in mind that a range that seems too wide – such as '20 to 60' – looks a bit dodgy and desperate, which may limit responses. Likewise, a range that's too narrow (one to two years) also seems odd. Even those who fall in it might not respond. Honesty is the best policy – stating your age, and avoiding ranges altogether, is regarded as the best approach.

6 Details, details. How many times have you read a personal ad that states: 'I enjoy movies, music, and going out'? This sentence describes most people! What you want is to make yourself stand out from the rest. So, name a recent movie you enjoyed. List some of your

favourite music styles, song titles, or artists. If you enjoy going out to Italian restaurants, or line-dancing at a country bar on Saturday nights, say so. Detail always provides a more accurate picture of you.

7 Honesty, again, is the best policy – not just about age, but about everything. No matter who you are, or what kind of person you are seeking, you have a better chance of finding that person – and with less disappointment along the way – if you are truthful from the outset.

Tips for replying…

Don't go for anything obviously sexual.

Do be inventive. *Time Out*'s favourite story is of a man who ran an ad asking for 'a chocolate factory heiress'. One respondent made up a fake packet of chocolates, each 'sweet' containing a different message about her. It may have taken some time, but she got a date! Use your glorious gut instincts (*see the next chapter*).

The Internet

I'm sick of being on my own. That's why the Internet is good. I talk to people on there. I'm on there every night that I'm home. And they're not necessarily potential dates. I've had hysterics on a chatline – sitting here on a Friday night absolutely hysterically laughing. I thought, 'God is this weird. I'm sitting here in front of a keyboard laughing with complete strangers on a screen'. It's very addictive though. Very addictive.

Joanne, on her online habit

Advantages: It's not restricted to your local area – it has the whole world in its hands. It's cheaper than an agency. It's new. It's exciting. It's easy (you don't even have to get dressed up to do it). People may be much more open via the written word than the spoken one. It feels safe chatting this way. You can even hide behind an anonymous cyber-name if you wish. You can terminate contact easily with anyone, anytime.

Disadvantages: You don't get to see who you're talking to. There is nothing and no one screening the responses you get. It can be more sexual than other avenues. It isn't governed by the guidelines there are for agencies. It can be addictive, and addictive is expensive. There are a lot of nutters out there.

This is by far and away the booming new way to make new friends, new relationships. The numbers are mind-boggling. One free dating site on the worldwide web boasted the following statistics:

Free ads placed here in the last 24 hours: 1,411

Searches performed in the last 24 hours: 72,000

Messages sent here in the last 24 hours: 6,817

Internet provider aol.com, for example, has seen 1200 weddings as a result of people meeting on its Love Shack site, set up on Valentine's Day 1996. Newspapers have been full of stories of long-distance lovers meeting via the Net and upping sticks to move to the other side of the world to live with people they haven't yet clapped eyes on. Like Katrina Gibbon, who met Canadian Paul Graham and decided to move sticks to Winnipeg just five days after their first Internet conversation. God knows how or why someone can be so sure when they haven't even seen another in the flesh, let alone slept together, but she was.

And these relationships can work. As one correspondant on a dating site puts it:

I met my husband, online, October 1997. I was in Minnesota, USA, he was in England. I moved here, June 12, 1998 and married him September last year. We were written up in the London Evening Standard. *It's working out well… but we took time, to get to know each other – eight months online and tons of phone calls. It can, and does work, with caution advised. They say, there's someone for everyone, you have to kiss a lot of frogs before you find your prince, or princess. No one's perfect, but the computer is one way of weeding out the yukkie ones. It beats hanging out at bars. Just exercise caution, be nice and you'll be surprised by just who you might meet.*

Good luck, Jen

So, if you wish to emulate Jen, here goes…

The good thing about the Internet is I can be very assertive in writing. They send me a photo and I say I'm very sorry but you're not my type, but I wish you good luck. Actually, there was one guy who so appreciated my honesty that we carried on talking. I ended up meeting up with him a couple of times but I was right. I didn't fancy him. But usually that's the end of it.

Here are the top tips from aol's agony aunt Matt Whyman and Internet counsellor Philippa Perry, who spend their lives dealing with cyberdates...

Do...

- Look for friends, not just dates. Philippa Perry advises: 'I wouldn't recommend just going online to date. If you're interested in classical music, join a classical music newsgroup. You'll be much more likely to meet someone you actually hit it off with. If you troll things like women for men newsgroups, that's where you're more likely to meet predatory men. A woman I know met a man on a fine art forum on compuserve. He came from Chicago, and now they're living together in St Albans.'
- Do use chatrooms as a 'meet market', but go into instant messaging (most Internet providers offer this service) as soon as you find someone you want to get to know better. It's confidential, and private. Matt Whyman says: 'If you're looking for a serious relation-

ship it's important to get it offline as soon as possible, so you don't waste time on the wrong people.'

- Practise. You can use the chatrooms to hone your cyberskills. Matt Whyman says: 'When you start using it at first it can be a bit hit and miss. It's quite good talking at first with, say, someone in LA and completely botching the relationship; then, when you're more confident, using UK chatrooms closer to home.'
- Be wary. The person you're talking to may not be all they seem. As Matt Whyman put it: 'The lovely-sounding guy from Birmingham might turn out to be a red-neck trucker from Georgia. Because people can use false names and even set up false profiles pretending they're from other countries, there is no way of telling. Plus there are an awful lot of married men out there. Also, I do a teen column and I get a lot of questions from young lads, like "I'm 14 and I met this girl online who's 25. I told her I'm 25, but now she's talking to me in ways I don't understand."'
- Get your relationship offline as soon as possible. Try and speak to them on the phone. Their voice – plus how they are about being phoned – will tell you a lot that the Internet disguises.
- Have fun. Philippa Perry says: 'Personally I get the most fun being myself. That's what works for me. Other people might have fun being fantasy figures and that might strike notes with someone else who likes that. For some people, being a fantasy figure is being themselves.'

- Read and stick to all the guidelines about meeting up in the dating agency section. Despite the fact you feel you know somebody intimately via e-mail, all the usual rules about letting friends know where you are, still apply. Even if you've had a cyber relationship for a month, you're still on a blind date.

Don't

- Give out your complete real name, address or phone number until you're really sure. Never give them out at the beginning. Matt Whyman says: 'If you can phone them from a payphone or mobile phone initially it's less likely to compromise you badly.'
- Dismiss people straight away. Philippa Perry points out: 'You might just not understand the rhythm of his writing or his particular style. Underneath he might be fantastic. Like in real life, prejudices can keep you lonely.'
- Don't assume you'll hit it off when you meet face-to-face. Matt Whyman says: 'The fact people are opening their heart to you is very flattering so when you meet in the real world and you don't know what to say to each other it can bring you crashing down. You have to keep an open mind and not assume it'll be as good as it is online.'

Finally there's the good old favourite…

Blind Dates

Advantages: Your friends know the kind of people you like. If you both like the same people, you already have something in common. And something to talk about. The service is completely free.
Disadvantages: Your friends may have a very strange idea of the kind of people you might like. You may feel embarrassed around your friends afterwards, especially if he's a bozo. Plus, numbers are limited and opportunities dry up after a while.

When You Actually Meet

For ordinary blind dates, dating agency dates, lonely hearts and cyberdates, the following rules about meeting up apply...

1. Once you receive the addresses and phone numbers for any contacts, telephone them in the first instance. If no phone number is given, write a short, friendly letter of introduction. Never visit someone without first having been invited.
2. Don't be put off by that old, 'but-I'm-a-woman-he-should-call-me' chestnut. Using agencies and ads sends

all those silly old rules flying out the window. Men who have advertised, or joined an agency, will be expecting women to call them.

3. Never call at unsociable hours (late at night or very early in the morning). Make sure you are speaking with the person you have been matched with, or who placed the ad. If anyone else answers the phone, be discreet. If you leave a message with someone (or on an answer-phone) please don't mention the dating agency or ad – some people share accommodation and may not want others to know about their private life.
4. If you hear from someone you feel is not quite what you're looking for, don't make the excuse that you're seeing someone. It is far kinder to be honest and say that you prefer not to take things any further, and wish them luck in their search.
5. You should answer all letters and return all calls. It is upsetting, having taken the trouble to write or call, not to receive a reply. Treat others as you would wish them to treat you.
6. Some people do 'click' immediately over the telephone, and whirlwind romances can happen; however it does make sense to have several telephone conversations or letters so that you know a little more about each other before you meet. Don't be put off if you're not immediately bowled over by someone – even the best relationships take a little time to develop.

7 You should arrange your first meeting in a public place, Dateline recommend an afternoon coffee or a brief lunchtime drink. Don't commit yourself to a long first date – an entire evening out could be a disaster if you don't get along.

8 Do make sure you get the full name and a telephone number for the person you're meeting, so that if you have problems getting to the date or need to reschedule it, you can let them know in advance.

9 Personal security is crucial – never invite someone to your home on a first date (or meet them at their home). Also don't accept a lift to or from the date – make your own way there and back, and make sure you have the money for public transport and/or taxis and know the times of trains or buses. It is also sensible to let someone know where you are going, who you are meeting (of course, you needn't mention you're dating someone through an agency or ad), and what time you expect to be home.

10 Before the date, do discuss dress code. It's embarrassing turning up in casual dress when your date has 'dressed up' or vice versa. Discuss it when you're arranging to meet up.

11 Above all, realize the person you are going to meet may also be nervous. SMILE – it's a great ice-breaker!

The Sod's Law of Love

or How you always meet someone when you're not looking

I have never, ever met a man at a party or where you're meant to meet them. Men have chatted me up in clubs, but I've never actually had a relationship with someone I met that way. With my longest-term boyfriend I was really happy being on my own and had been for 18 months, I'd even just been on my first ever holiday with a girlfriend. I came back feeling brilliant about myself and I swear meeting a man was the last thing on my mind. I was with a gang of people and when I saw him in the pub, I thought, 'that's a nice looking man', and then, 'that's something I've not thought about for a long time'.

Then later when I went to art college, it never occurred to me I'd meet the man of my dreams or that it would be full of single men. It was a complete shock to me when a gorgeous guy started flirting with me. I thought, I'm here to do art, not talk to boys. My experience is it's when you're getting on with your own life, you meet someone. A friend of mine had always wanted a house of her own, but waited years and didn't move from her flat because she thought, I can't have a house until I meet the man I want to spend my life with. Eventually she gave up and bought a house. Two weeks later she met this man at work without even trying, having been to every party for years, just in case. I do really think you meet the best men when you're going about your business.

Leah, agreeing with the folk wisdom that you meet him when not looking

It's a very popular piece of folk wisdom indeed. And anecdotal evidence does back it up. Although, anecdotal evidence also backs up the thousands of couples who do meet via agencies, the Internet and so on. Given the lack of sound research on the subject, you take your pick as to what to believe. Bearing in mind it's never a bad thing to be getting on with your own life anyway…

CHAPTER 20

Your Glorious Gut Instincts

I went out with somebody last week I met through the Internet. He sent me his photo and I didn't like the look of him but he had a Harley Davidson and I adore bikes so I thought: 'Maybe, let's give it a go, it's just a night out'.

I got there on time and he was late so I saw him arriving and thought... 'Oh, shit'.

I hadn't listened to my gut instinct which had told me he sounded like a boring old anally retentive fart. And he was. The Harley was a wild card.

We had a meal which was a mistake because it was two hours – too long. He said he'd give me a lift home and I thought OK – at least I get to try out the Harley. We got back to my flat and I said thank you very much, take care. I started to walk away and he said 'Will I see you again?' and I said 'No I'm sorry but thank you.' And that was that. I feel so much better when I'm more open and honest.

Lola, 32, on the perils of ignoring those basic instincts

How do you know whether someone you meet via the Internet is really worth dating? Or whether someone you meet in a bar is someone you'd appreciate in the cold light of day?

Thankfully you have a very powerful tool at your disposal which never lets you down – should you choose to use it. It is your gut instinct, your female intuition. Call it what you will, it works. And it works for you.

Think of your past dating disasters. In the vast majority of cases you'll be able to remember some clue, some pointer as to the kind of person you'd met.

Once, on a first date, a friend told her date she was about to go off on a business trip abroad. Suddenly his face darkened and he said 'Oh, I know what those trips are like. I suppose you'll end up shagging someone out there.' Understandably she took offence at his foul slander on her character. Years later she looked back on this as a first clue of his jealousy, possessiveness, lack of trust and controlling behaviour.

The good thing about your gut instinct is the more you use it, the stronger it gets. And the way to use it is to listen to it, to become aware of how your gut instinct manifests itself.

It may be that you just don't like the look of him when he turns up. It may come to you as a creeping feeling that this just won't work. You may find yourself feeling angry. It may register via certain clues – like you notice he's not listening to you, or keeps interrupting you. His eyes may keep moving away from your face as he speaks. Or he may be so practised at the art of flirting that a little suspicious voice in you peeps: 'This all sounds a little off pat. I think he's said all this many times before.'

I had one of those, once. On our first date he said: 'Tell me your favourite taste, your favourite touch, sight, smell, sounds'. It was all terribly sensual, romantic and, frankly, a turn-on. When we came to the end of the meal he hollered, 'Waiter, give me the bill so I can take this woman outside and kiss her!' Yet my gut instinct was flashing a warning message which said: This may feel terribly exciting but there's something up. There's something cold, something rehearsed about it all. It's like he's acting and doesn't really *feel* as romantic, as entranced, as he's sounding. Lo and behold my gut was right. Mr Chat turned out to be a serial seducer. I'm sure he *has* used those lines on countless women.

A body language expert once told me our gut instincts are actually our brain cells making a connection with our knowledge bank about people and behaviour. If you've seen Saddam Hussein on TV, you've seen a psychopath in action and somewhere in your brain you remember that. Then when you meet someone in a bar and they start doing something that reminds you on some level of Saddam Hussein on TV your brain registers – Aha! Psychopath!

Even so, we are also expert at ignoring the messages we receive. I've done that so often it's amazing my poor neglected intuition kept going. What happened is my mind kicked in to diss my gut instinct the minute it started working, with rationalizations like… 'oh, he's all right really'. 'He's probably nervous'. 'He's got an interesting job so I'll give him another chance'. With husband no. 2 I managed to ignore my gut instincts until after the wedding!

Yet they were there. Gut instincts are a fact. We all have them. And they're a valuable asset which work even with people you meet on the Internet. As Joanne, after two years of intrepid dating, says:

You just kind of know. If someone e-mails you or you meet in a chatroom, and it's all about sex and they can't talk about anything else, you know that's all they want. Even on e-mail you can tell people's moods. It's quite interesting. You just kind of have a feeling. The other day, this guy sent me an instant message that said 'Hi, are you into swinging?' I said 'No, why?' And I thought, if you're into swinging you're with a partner. We carried on talking. I looked at his profile and it said we are interested in so and so. So I asked him if he was married he said 'No, separated'. He sent me a photo and he looked OK. We carried on talking a few times. We spoke on the phone and arranged to meet for lunch but I thought, I don't know, there's something about this that doesn't feel right. So the next night I used a different name and sent him an instant message that said 'Hi, do you want to talk?' And he got talking about swinging again. In this other persona I said, 'Are you married?' And he said 'Yes'. I said 'Does your wife mind?' He said 'No, we love each other'. And I'm thinking, you bastard. So I thought why meet him? I don't want to go with a married man.

Of course, it's easy to get feelings of 'No, he's wrong' muddled with general nervousness. Which is why, unless your instincts are *screaming*, it's important to give someone a chance. If he keeps glancing away it may be because he's nervous. Trust your feeling on this. It's what female intuition is for. If you're not sure, give them the benefit of the doubt and meet up again, but if you *are* sure, you are.

How You Can Strengthen your Basic Instincts

WHAT TO DO:

- Think about your past loves and the information you had at the very beginning. Think about how that information came to you. Was it something he said? The way he looked? A general feeling you had? What triggered warning bells? Or, if he was lovely, what was it about him that told you, this man's for me? We all receive our gut messages in different ways depending on whether we're primarily people who work visually, or by what we hear, or feel. Knowing how your messages come to you helps you tune the frequency so they issue through loud and clear.
- Remember it's not what he says, it's what he *does* that counts. Actions really do speak louder than words. So if he says he'll call, then doesn't, or says he wants a

relationship with you, then starts flirting with every woman in the joint, be suspicious. Is his behaviour consistent? Is he ambiguous? Does he commit to anything and follow it through? What does he say about his past relationships? Are you making all the effort?

- If there's someone you're interested in now, think how the approach happened between you. Did they come on forcefully, impulsively? With a joke or in deadly earnest? Did you sit there passively while someone approached you? Or was it you who went striding across the gym to seek out your quivering quarry? Psychotherapists often start relationships workshops by getting people to pair up and then talk about *how* the pairing-up happened, because it always provides a blueprint for how things will progress.
- How open is he? A very good way of judging people is to notice how willing they seem to be to get involved or how detached they seem. Wanting to get involved shows up via lots of facial expressions – nodding, smiling, and makings lots of um-hum noises. Also, encouraging you to talk. Moreover, they answer when you ask them questions! They do not avoid or use evasion tactics like changing the subject.If they appear very distant and are playing it cool, it may of course show passionate depths – but it's going to be harder to reach them. Someone who is relaxed and comfortable with themselves will have a relaxed, open stance. And if they mirror your body language and movements – they like you!

Our body movements are usually reliable indicators of our intentions. So when someone moves closer they usually want to be more intimate; when they lean back or turn sideways, they want out!

Ones to watch:

Doesn't make much eye contact:
They're either detached, uninterested or plain shifty.
Stare piercingly at you:
Control freak.
Arms tightly crossed:
They're on the defensive.
They look away:
They're bored. Either they don't like you, or they do like you but they have the attention span of an amphetamine-fuelled gnat.
Twitchy jerky movements:
Uptight, maybe even on drugs, (especially if combined with enlarged pupils). Although it could be down to stress or too much coffee.
In a man, hips thrust to one side, hands pointing downwards to genitals:
This, apparently, is a sure sign of a womaniser.
Staring into your eyes, staring at your mouth, listening very intently, oodles of charm:
Could be the casanova type. Often these types use a huge amount of humour which is actually a smokescreen so you don't get really close to them.

Rearranging the cutlery, picking fluff off the carpet: Control freak, again. Will also have a very orderly appearance, and will want everything just so around them. They will place the drinks on the coasters, push the dirty ashtray away.

Can You Tell If Someone's Lying?

Body language expert Phillippa Davis says:

If their hands move to the face – little gestures around the face, like touching quickly the mouth or nose, can indicate someone's lying. Also eyes moving away too quickly or too quick a response and the voice pitch moving up a bit. Also, liars overdo it in terms of information. They put in too much detail. Like, 'I did not have an affair with that woman Miss Lewinsky'. We all know who that woman *is.*

CHAPTER 21

The Scientifically Proven, Psychologically Sound First Date

I love the whole theatre of dating. Of getting all dressed up. Of seeing him all sweaty and nervous and playing on it. Going out for a meal just to flirt and kiss. I'd much rather do that than be in a relationship, not because I'm a horrible tease but because I don't enjoy waking up with a man unless I really like him because people aren't so great in the morning.

Maria, dating enthusiast

I met my husband at 16, so I didn't get to date as a teenager. I realized when I was single that this was what I needed to do. It got to the stage where I thought I have to do things differently, I have to try things I haven't done before. And I was absolutely terrified. Because a relationship was what I really, really wanted, the whole thing seemed so loaded. Eventually it was my daughter who told me, you have to lighten up, Mum, it isn't the most important thing. She reminded me how when she was young I taught her to really value herself and not give herself away. Now she was telling me the same thing, and I thought, blimey, I'd better do it then. Once I changed my attitude, I realized what a laugh dating can be.

Therese, dating trainee

These women are at opposite ends of the nervousness spectrum when it comes to a first date. Not everyone feels as confident as Maria or as nervous as Therese. You probably fall between the two. Wherever you are, as we said in Chapter 16, it does help to think of a date as no big deal.

If, however, for you it is, be easy on yourself. Use your judgement as to how much of a state you need to be in.

And, remember, you're always going to experience some element of nerves. As Pam Bathe of Dateline puts it: 'A certain frisson adds a je ne sais quoi to the meeting. It would be awfully sad if we ever became blasé.'

Remember, he's doubtless nervous too.

You may feel like you're competing in the date Olympics where the judges – or, rather, judge – is studying your every move, deciding whether to award you a medal or disqualify you from further heat. So there's a temptation to put on your best performance, to believe that one slip and you've failed. But everyone from psychologists to seasoned daters say that putting on an act is a hiding to disaster. The best way to handle a first date is:

BE YOURSELF

If you're a bubbly personality, bubble. If you're normally quiet, shut up.

Know yourself – do you get really nervous? Or couldn't care less. Know which is you and look after yourself.

Before the Date

Therese (above) coped with her anxiety on date days by talking to friends, telling them about her nerves and asking people about what she should wear. And by making sure what she did wear made her feel good and comfortable.

Remember to remind yourself: **'I'm not here to make this work, but to see if I like this person or not. If it doesn't feel good, I won't do it again'.**

Do...

- Take Rescue Remedy (available from most chemists and health shops). Or have a relaxing aromatherapy bath or burn some oils. Or take a homoeopathic remedy to calm your nerves. (Ask at a pharmacy, or find a local homoeopath)
- And use your affirmations. Whenever you feel a bat-squeak of nerves emerging, say one or some of these to yourself...

  I am a gorgeous, sexy woman and any man would be lucky to have me
  Today I am confident, witty, funny, clear/whatever...
  I am calm, confident and comfortable with myself
  Whatever happens, I'll handle it
  It's OK for me to flirt and be attractive
  I am lovable

I am attracting a healthy, loving relationship
It's OK for me to be on a date
This is just a coffee with a man

- Focus in on whatever's making you nervous. If it's your looks, tell yourself you're gorgeous. If it's your ability to sustain a conversation, tell yourself you're funny, clear, direct, talkative. If it's fear of being hurt, tell yourself whatever happens, you'll handle it. If it's fear of dating per se, tell yourself it's no big deal, just a coffee and you have cupfuls of confidence.

What to Wear

The irony of wardrobe. It's the thing women most agonize over, and the thing men most ignore. In an *Esquire* magazine survey, dress sense came out ninth on a list of men's attributes of the ideal woman – after a good figure, face, humour, legs, eyes, breasts, bottom and intelligence.

Do...

- Wear something you're comfortable in, something you don't have to keep hitching, pulling, twisting or checking. One experienced dater advises: 'I like to wear clothes I feel sexy in. That's doesn't mean low cut or revealing but an outfit I know I look good in.'

- Discuss dress code with your date. If he has chosen where you're going, ask him what kind of thing would be appropriate.

Don't...

- Go over the top. Dress *down*, if anything. If you're too smart you'll feel uncomfortable; if you're dressed too provocatively you may give him the wrong message (or not, as the case may be!). Show him your mind, not your body.

Where to Go

The cinema

There's a saying that if a man takes you here on a first date, he's interested in only one thing and it isn't conversation. Or the film. However, a movie does give you something neutral to talk about afterwards. The downside is you spend two hours sitting awkwardly beside someone you hardly know, trying to concentrate.

But, apparently, a horror or a stirring story can be perfect. US scientists carried out an experiment where men were put in scary situations then met by a female research assistant for assessment. The men who were most frightened or stressed invariably rated the female most favourably and were most likely to call her up after the experiment for a date. So exploit the emotional potential of getting scared out of your wits and grabbing one another for comfort…

Lunch

Is a can't-lose choice. It has an end that isn't too far from the beginning if he's dull as dishwater. And can linger on all afternoon if he has the looks of Ewan McGregor and the entertainment value of Harry Hill.

A walk

Has the advantage of burning off nervous tension. Plus moving about maximizes a crucial difference between the sexes – while women bond by talking, men bond by doing something. If you're both sporty types, you can take this even further by taking action. Play tennis, go horseriding, even canoeing. Then you can bond about it afterwards and take advantage of the fact research also suggests men feel fruitier and see women as more attractive after physical exertion.

Do…

Make sure you arrive on time (or call to say you are running late). You'll only make yourself – and him – anxious if you're late.

Don't…

Do anything you feel uncomfortable with. If physical activity beyond raising a fork to your lips fills you with terror rather than just-enough-stress-to-be-sexy, forget it and go see a film. And never agree to anything you don't really want to do. Apart from anything else, it gives him the wrong messages about you.

Turn up with anyone else. Especially your children.

Dinner

Dinner or a drink are the most common choices for first forays – you get to know one another, there's the distraction of the food/bar, it's neutral territory and you can have a drink to ease the tension.

Do...

- Make a suggestion. Men hate being the ones who always have to choose where to go.
- Look after yourself. If you have had problems with food and eating makes you tense, don't do it. Similarly if you can't stand alcohol, don't agree to a drink.

Don't...

- Criticize his mistakes. If he gets soup on his chin, or the place serves food you wouldn't give your cat, don't make a fuss. Overlook his blunders, slips and spills; make light of them and he'll love you forever.
- Get drunk! Yes, we've all done it. And nerves don't help, but getting paralytic on a first outing can lead you to say – and do – certain things you may later regret. I know, I once got pickled on a first date and asked the

man whether he wanted children and if so did he want them with me.

What to say

Whether your first date is shopping at Tesco or tea at the Ritz the only thing that matters is you both give good talk.

Do…

- Offer him a compliment. Often the first thing a man says on a first date is 'Like the dress'. If he doesn't, he should. Yet how often do we return the compliment? One of the men I interviewed said: 'I hate how we're expected to make all the effort. If a woman compliments me it says three things. It tells me she's confident, she's nice and not a frosty ice maiden and, most importantly, she's keen, which puts me at my ease'.
- Be yourself. If he mentions his first from Cambridge don't start making out you're a great intellectual yourself. If it sounds like he spends his whole life following Arsenal don't feign an interest in sport you don't feel. If he doesn't like you for who you are, he isn't right for you.
- Tell him you're nervous (if you are). As we know from part one, speaking your feelings helps to make them go away. And if he admits to nerves too, you'll feel closer

to one another. If he responds by trying to make you *more* nervous, well, you know then what to think of *him*.

- Ask him how he thinks and feels. The two questions: 'Oh, yes and how do you feel about that?' and 'What do you think about that?' can reveal bucketloads about your potential mate. On a first date, I once asked a man how he felt about something that had happened to him and he answered: 'I don't know. I never know what I'm feeling.' He was right. And I was about to discover it's not easy having a relationship with someone who never knows if they're angry or ecstatic.
- Touch him. Touching establishes intimacy, demonstrates warmth and presumes familiarity. Which is a wonderful cure for first-night nerves.
- Listen!

Don't...

- Bombard him with questions that point to an above-average interest in whether he'll make a good life partner. Show an interest, but don't be too nosy or intrusive too soon. Some bright, confident women can frighten men to death.
- Talk, talk, talk. It's a feminine trait, especially when nervous, to yak as though you were practising for the European Yakking Championships. But how are you going to find out about *him*?

- Mention the M word, as in, 'Last Saturday I went to my sister's wedding.'
- Be frightened of silence.
- Rattle on about exes. Remember the *Friends* episode where Rachel on a first date chattered incessantly about how she was over Ross? It is not a good idea to mention ex-partners, particularly by name. It makes your date feel inadequate.
- Tell him your entire past history. Especially your relationship past history. He'll feel overwhelmed, and it'll probably bring up painful feelings for you so you feel awkward. Keep it light.
- Moan about your job, your life, your family and especially your exes. Now is the time to accentuate the positive.

And never, ever use this phrase: *I'm no good with men.*

This phrase – and others like it – is entirely banned from your vocabulary around anyone you find attractive. Running yourself down won't make you feel good and it won't make him feel good about you thus becoming a self-fulfilling prophecy.

Who Pays?

Do…

- Offer. My friend Sue says: 'I actually think men should pay on a first date – especially if he asked you. But I always offer to go halves. If he says, no, you can pay next time, it's lovely.'
- Suggest 'I'll pay next time'. But only if it's going well.

Don't…

- Insist on paying or going halves. There is some primitive part of a man's brain that likes to demonstrate he can be a provider. So let him.
- Make some half-hearted excuse along 'I left my purse at home' lines. It makes you look cheap – and less than honest.

The Coffee Dilemma

To ask him in after, or not to ask him in after, that is the question. Especially when coffee famously does not necessarily mean a hot beverage.

No...

- If you don't feel entirely safe with him, if you're dog tired or you want to keep him dangling like a panting puppy.

Yes...

- Some women say this is the only time the pair of you actually start to relax. But you do have to be very careful. One first date I invited in, who'd seemed the perfect gentleman in the restaurant, walked straight up to the bedroom and wouldn't come down until I threatened to call the cops.

Don't...

- Feel pressurized into sex. Sex on a first date is OK only if *you* feel the time is right.

Negotiating a Second Date

Do...

- Go for it! If you've had a wonderful time and your gut instinct tells you he has too, spare yourself the stress of obsessing afterwards about whether or not he liked you and grasp the nettle. Try saying I had a really nice time. And if he doesn't take the hint, add: 'Shall we see one another again?' or 'Would you like to see me again?'

(like it's a big privilege, not like you're desperate). If he's vague, then you know it hasn't gone as well as you think. But at least you know. And if he says yes, you'll feel wonderful.

Don't...

- Say it in a scary, needy, graspy way, as in 'Are you free tomorrow?'
- Play it too cool if you really like him. Chances are he'll take your ice queen act as rejection and disapper quicker than an ice pixie.

Afterwards

Do...

- Give him a second chance. The stress, nerves and expectations of a first date can make people do some peculiar things. Nervousness can make men talk all the time, the desire to impress can make some men appear arrogant and boastful. Unless he's a complete dork, men, like cars and houses, benefit from a second viewing.
- Use your gut instincts (*see Chapter 20, page 262*) to decide which you're dealing with.

Don't...

- Go into a hole if it went badly. It is not the end of the world. Even if you liked him and it evidently wasn't reciprocated, at least you've found out now, not ten years down the track and with only a few hours of your precious time wasted.
- Judge him according to what your friends/parents/children would think of him. It's you who's going to be seeing him in his socks.
- Start choosing your bridesmaids or planning your children's schools. Keep expectations down to a minimum. These are very early days. All the women I talked to had had the experience of a perfect first date where the date never called again.

First Date Disasters

If it was a dozo, console yourself with the fact it may not have been as bad as these:

'He was half an hour late and turned up with his best friend who insulted me – when I said I worked in a bank he said, "You look like you'd do something boring like that" – and bombarded me with questions as though he was a chaperone sussing me out for his friend. I felt furious, and wished to God I'd had *my* best friend there to even the odds. Believe it or not, mug that I am, I dated him twice after that, and I realized he wasn't interested in a relationship at all really. Which was kind of symbolized by his bringing his mate along on a first date.'

'I was so nervous with this guy, because I really liked him. But when we went out, I discovered he was a bit of a drinker, I'm not. However, I stupidly felt I had to keep up with him. I was doing OK, then suddenly felt really drunk when we got outside the restaurant. Then – horror of horrors – I threw up all over him in the taxi home. Needless to say, he didn't call me again. And I was way too embarrassed to call him.'

'He spent the entire time constantly looking over his shoulder at other women. Then he had the cheek to ask me what I thought of one of them – a particularly stunning blonde. I just said "We obviously have nothing in common", stood up and walked out.'

'We were having a drink and a whole lot of people came over who he recognized and he didn't introduce me. I thought, that's a bit rude. I said so, and he said "I'm really sorry, I forgot your name". It wasn't a good sign.'

'We were getting on really well and he said "I find you really easy to talk to", which was nice and made me feel good. Then he told me he was in love with his ex and knew he would never feel that way about another woman. My face must have dropped and he said, "Sorry, I needed to talk to someone about it and because you're so understanding..."'

'It was all going swimmingly, then he told me I was of the wrong religion and he'd sworn to himself he'd never date a non-Jewish woman. Which rather begged the question: why did you ask me out then? I felt completely deflated, and the conversation just kind of died after that.'

And the winner is...

'We went for a coffee and to begin with he was OK. Then he said let's go to the park. It was a sunny day and we were walking along and he produced this Walkman, and got me to listen to music he's made with his mates. Then he seemed to crumble up into a state of high anxiety and rushed off to the shop, leaving me listening to mad loud rock music. He came back with loads of beer and at the same time is telling me he's a recovering alchoholic and just out of rehab for crack cocaine addiction. This isn't going too well, I thought. I'd better have a beer myself.

'He had one beer and it was like someone had clicked a switch and he morphed into this complete nutter. He said you're the woman of my dreams. I think you're amazing and we could live happily ever after. This is within two hours. Then he launched into this story about how he had this incredible penis. "I can take a woman to another dimension".

'He got more and more drunk and I said, "This has been fun, but I'm going to go now."

'He grabbed my hand and said "You're not going anywhere". I was really scared he'd chase me down the street or something. I'd had a drink too and I wasn't really thinking straight. I suggested we went to a pub so I could dodge out easier.

'Then he took a call on his mobile and it sounded to me like he was making a drugs deal. He was muttering, "a hundred, a hundred, meet me in Leicester Square". I stood up in the pub and said I wasn't having it. He said "I wasn't buying drugs, I was buying you jewellery because I love you."

'So I gathered my stuff together, and said this date is over. He followed me all the way to the station, shouting at me all along the road. When I got home there were nine answerphone messages from him. I had to change my number to stop him calling me.'

CHAPTER 22

How's it Going?

I just started seeing someone new but before I had been on and off single for two years. Previously I had been with a guy for seven years.

I felt like I got over that in a weekend. Now I'm feeling like I'm dealing with a lot of things I didn't deal with when I was single. I feel almost commitment phobic. I was in Sainsbury's the other day and I virtually had a panic attack thinking, I ought to buy him some Crunchy Nut Cornflakes so he can have breakfast at my place before he leaves for work in the morning. But I can't possibly *buy food I don't eat myself. There are a lot of things I don't want to get back into. Like not having to tune the radio off Kiss fm to Radio 4 every five minutes. I'm thinking of buying duplicate radios and turning one on and one off. And I have real problem with James's underwear hanging around here. I feel mean handing it back to him, but I do. I loved being single. I think I'll have real trouble building a relationship because I've been basically spoilt, just pleasing myself.*

Maria, on the trials of doing it all again

How are you?

As a very wise woman said, when I was researching this book, love brings out anything that is not like itself. If you find a nice, loving, available man, you might be ecstatic. And you might find yourself going to pieces.

If you do, don't worry. It's natural. Especially if you have been hurt in the past.

Love can provoke old hurts that still need healing. When Rosa got together with Andrew, she found herself awash with all manner of emotions. She says:

It was weird. I was very happy, I was very grateful I'd finally found the kind of relationship I wanted. And it was very scary – and tricky for him (and for me being with him) because he was happy with me and I was sad a lot of the time. I felt sad for all the time wasted; self-pity for all the energy wasted; anger at having put up with difficult people; and fear of being truly open and intimate and therefore vulnerable.

Which goes to show how dating again and new relationships bring up feelings. And not just those fizzy, whizzy, in-love feelings but, occasionally, more decidedly plonky, difficult-to-deal-with feelings. Usually feelings you thought you'd dealt with.

There are a myriad of ways dating again can stir up the emotional pot:

Opening up to someone again, being vulnerable, laying yourself open to having your feelings hurt can bring up fear.

Someone finally being lovely to you can bring up anger about loves who weren't.

Talking about the past with someone new, as you inevitably do, can bring any unhealed hurts rising to the surface.

Having someone demanding your time – and cupboard space for their crunchy nut cornflakes – can bring up irritability and resentment. Especially when you have been single and *loved* it.

Having sex again can remind you of the last one you got that close with. Or the one you've never quite got over. It may not be as good as it was with *him*. Or it may be better and bring up sadness about how you put up with so little for so long.

Having sex again can bring up any insecurity about your body and how it looks. It hits on all your issues and unhelpful beliefs around relating and sex. Like ambivalence about whether you really enjoy sex. Or your beliefs about whether you really, really deserve love.

And all this can bring up feelings of being uncomfortable with yourself because, traditionally, this should be a happy, rose-tinted time. Not a time when old ghosts come back to haunt you.

What You Can do

- Hopefully, after reading and working with Chapter 3 and Chapter 13 you now have more skills for looking after yourself emotionally. Acknowledge to yourself, him and others that you're still in a vulnerable state.
- Talk to friends, write it all down in your journal, but most of all, talk to him about how you're feeling. It may be scary, but it will help it pass quicker. And do you really want a relationship where you can't communicate difficult feelings and get them supported?
- Remember you can take things as fast or slow as you wish. You are responsible for 50 per cent of the relationship. You have 50 per cent of the say as to when and how you see one another and how often. You could even make a list of what you want to retain of your single life in your newly non-single state. Like Maria who says, 'Before I was single I thought my natural state was to be in a relationship; but now friends say you were so natural as a couple, and now you're so natural as a single. That's such a compliment. And now I feel hugely reluctant to let go of control over my life and my arrangements and myself. I don't like my new boyfriend arranging to meet me too far in advance and when I was doing my relationship commandments the other day and I had one which was I have to be by

myself at least three days a week, I can't be doing with being with someone every night.'

How is He?

I've lived on my own for 14 months and in that time I have created a really lovely home, which has been a sanctuary for me to heal myself in. I would be very reticent just to let anyone in here. I would like a man in my life; but also there are lots of aspects about being single I really relish: like the lack of compromise, and the fact that being single has allowed me to explore lots of different areas of myself and my life. So I wouldn't give up my single status readily. I think I would negotiate a relationship very differently now I've been on my own. There are things I would want to maintain for myself, like nights out with single friends, time for myself, on my own. I also think I'm clearer about what I'm looking for. It isn't just any man, but someone who will value me.

Kate, on how single and loving it makes you choosier

So, forget, for a moment, am I all right to have a relationship? Is *he* all right for you?

If you're not sure, here are some questions to ask yourself about him:

Is he nice to me?

Do I feel comfortable when I'm with him?

Does my body feel comfortable with him – or am I tense?
Do I feel I can be completely myself with him?
Does he embarrass me?
Can I imagine introducing him to my friends?
Does he put me down? Allow me my own opinions?
Do I violently disagree with anything he says?
Do I like listening to him?
Is he listening to me?
Is he doing all the talking?
Is he difficult to talk to?
Is he drinking/taking drugs too much?
Have I any warning bells?
Does he share the same values/beliefs as me?
What do my glorious gut instincts say?
If I do have any reservations, given no one is perfect, are they liveable with or are they scary?

Blame it on the way we're brought up. Or that while little girls are nurturing their dolls, little boys are running all round the playground. We're brought up to focus on someone else; they're brought up to focus on what they want.

Rules:
It should it feel comfortable.

You have the right to be treated with care and respect. **And if it doesn't feel comfortable and you're not being treated with respect ... La Dumpcracha.**

WHAT IF HE DOESN'T CALL?

A frequent post-date anxiety. A frequent post-date reality.

Do you care? Do you really want a man where you have to be worrying about him all the time? Where he doesn't have the consideration to call when he says he will or call and say he's had a nice time.

As a piece of behaviour, not calling says, plainly and simply that he doesn't want/need/desire to talk with you. Or, as Joey in *Friends* puts it: 'Why do you have to break up with her? Be a man. Just stop calling.'

This happened to Therese after she had amazing sex after a hot date. No word for two weeks. Eventually, she called him. She got the information she needed. She laid it to rest in her own head and got to tell him what she thought of him. Which wasn't much.

Recognising What's Not Right and Ending it

The gentle art of La Dumperacha

What became easier and easier over time was ending the short relationships I'd have. Dates would fizzle out. You'd be having dinner and then you wouldn't. There wasn't any relationship to discuss. There was this guy in the summer I went out for a few dates, we had a nice time, he was sweet. One day we had a misunderstanding over the phone. He was on his mobile and I said, 'I can't hear you, the line's breaking up'. He thought I said 'I can't bear you, we're breaking up'. After that he didn't call and I didn't think to enquire why. I only heard later from a mutual friend that's what he thought happened. One crackly phone call later and you're not going out anymore and I didn't really care. That's what would happen.

Maria, expert at the art of goodbye

Unfortunately, not all dates fizzle out or softly roll over and die after some minor communication glitch. Some short relationships have to be prised apart like a barnacle and the bottom of a boat. Or a limpet and whatever it is a limpet sticks to.

If you're the one being dumped and your heart is hurting, go back and have a read of part one. But if you're the one doing the dumping, there are a few pointers that can make the whole thing a little easier.

- The main tactic to minimize your feeling like a heel – and him feeling like a worthless piece of carpet fibre – is to keep the focus on you. And tell the truth.
- Say something like one of these tried-and-tested end lines:

  'I realize this isn't working for me. I've had a lovely

time with you/you're a lovely man/ I really care about you and I'm choosing not to take it any further.'

'The attraction I felt for you isn't developing into anything deeper.'

'I'm choosing not to do this anymore.'

These statements all take responsibility for your choice, and takes it all off him being a terrible person or it being in any way his fault.

He may argue, manipulate, whinge, lose his temper, storm out, cry, start instantly flirting with someone else. Just be aware that's what he's doing and be aware you're sticking to your guns.

Remember:

You are not responsible for his feelings.
You have the right to say no and to end anything that isn't working for you.
You have the right to spend your time as you see fit.

But if all else fails, again, be a man. Just stop calling.

CHAPTER 23

Recognizing Mr Right

7 signs you've found the love of your life

'When you know, you know – that's what I've been told all my life – and now I know.'

Thus *Titanic* star Kate Winslet described meeting the love of her life in the shape of husband Jim Threapleton, who she met on the set of *Hideous Kinky*. 'I knew instantly… instantly. I thought: "Yep, I'll have that".'

You don't have to be a movie star to have such dramatic love-at-first-sight experiences. Ms Winslet is simply speaking for the hundreds of women who go through a remarkably similar process when encountering 'The One'.

And ironically, apart from the instant drama of eyes meeting across a crowded film set, hooking up with True Love seems to be accompanied by a distinctly down-to-earth sense of oh, right. Less: *This is it*!!!! More: this is it, then. On with the rest of our lives…

The women I talked to with 'I met the love of my life' experiences came up with remarkably similar factors which help you tell whether the one you're with is 'The One' or merely 'One Other'.

Recognizing Mr Right – 7 Ways to Tell

It's instant

Eyes meet across a crowded room. Something goes boom and life is never the same. Petruska Clarkson is a professor of counselling, psychology and psychotherapy. She says:

I'm a psychologist and a scientist and I never really believed in things like love at first sight but I had to change my mind because it actually happened to me. My husband fell in love with me at first sight. He was sitting in a dining room full of people. I came into the room (he'd never met me before) and he shouted *'yes!' I was so shocked and embarrassed I turned around and walked straight out. Later on, we started talking and I found we had many interests in common, like science, philosophy, psychology and art. We became very good friends. Then, after my partner started sleeping around with my students, I commenced my relationship with the man I met in that room. We've been married seven years and we're still in love and it's all very beautiful and lustful. It's a magnificent love story. And what would possess a person to say yes like that?*

Often, when Cinderella meets Prince Charming, one partner recognizes the attraction more quickly than the other. And they might have to chase their quarry half way round fairyland until the slower partner catches on. Even so, usually the other partner will be aware of *something*.

You feel like you've known each other forever

When Sally, 34, met Harry, sorry, Peter, she said 'Although I fancied him too, the main feeling was I'd met some long-lost brother.'

This is a very common feeling of deep unconscious ease when you hit on Mr Right.

Professor Clarkson agrees. She says: 'A significant feeling is that you've known them all your life and you don't have to explain a thing. When my husband first said "How are you?" I felt like he *really* cared, he was *really* interested. It wasn't just what could he get from me.'

It's comfortable

One friend says when she met her husband it was like glimpsing the most amazingly beautiful stilettoes ever, slipping her feet in and finding they fit like the comfiest slippers a toe ever wiggled in. She married him three months later and is still there five years on, now firmly convinced by the comfy stilettoes theory.

All the women I spoke to for this chapter agreed with her.

Rosa says: 'When I met Martin it was like having a new best girlfriend, but with a willy. I felt I could talk to him about anything, tell him anything, and he'd understand me.'

This feeling of comfort is not the same as the uncomfortable comfort you feel when you met someone who fits your lovemap but hits on old wounds. It's a deep contentment, an ease, which prompts Rosa to say: 'If I'd known it was meant to be this easy and smooth and glowy, I wouldn't have bothered with any of the others.'

It's no big drama

Which brings us to the 'it's no soap but it's lovely and bubbly' aspect of The Right One. Ironically, given the significance of having finally found a relationship that fits like Cinderella's slipper, there doesn't seem to be much to say about it.

Sally's past relationships have been fraught with angst and the kind of 'Do you think he likes me?/You'll never guess what he's done *now*' conversations that the writer of *Sex and the City* calls 'freaking'. Now she's met a lovely man she says: 'I'm not saying much because there's nothing *to* say. It's just normal. It's *weird* it's so normal, but it's normal.'

And Leah agrees:

Yes, it just feels kind of normal. I just felt like saying, 'Oh well, here we are then'. There was no big thunderclap. Yes, it was passionate. And it felt like something I'd been waiting for had finally arrived. People said you'll know when it happens and I did, in a really non-dramatic way. A week after we met he said I'm not interested in just sleeping with somebody, I want to be having a relationship with the person I'm sleeping with, what do you think. I said, yes, fine. And it just felt right. Not even, to be honest, particularly exciting. Just right.

It felt taken as read that we liked each other that much. Even when we told each other we loved one another it was a bit oh. *He said it in passing in the kitchen. And it was so easy I started thinking maybe he didn't say it. Perhaps he said get the beans and I didn't hear him right. But he did say it, and he's said it many times since. But I never felt like ringing someone up and saying* 'Guess what?'.

The Timing's Right

Rosa, above, reckons she had to be ready to notice Mr Right: 'I definitely felt quite calm and sorted. I had a feeling I would meet somebody, it felt like the right time. Although you go through life telling yourself you never know what will happen, you might meet someone at any moment, I also know I just wasn't ready for it before. I was too desperate, less happy with myself.'

The experts agree that lasting love is more of a possibility at some points in our lives than others. Dr Dean Ornish, US heart disease expert who writes of the heart in a broader sense in his new book *Love and Survival – The Scientific Basis for the Healing Power of Intimacy* (Vermillion) says: 'I am not saying that the key to happiness is finding the right Cinderella or Prince Charming, getting married and living happily ever after. Until I had done enough work on my own obstacles to intimacy, I was incapable of being in an intimate relationship with anyone, no matter who they were. It was not about *finding* the right person, it was about *being* the right person. I knew my beloved for a long time before we got into a relationship, but I couldn't even see her fully at the time.'

So, factors that influence readiness seem to be: you're the right age, you've had enough running around getting nowhere, you know yourself and you've grown up sufficiently not to give someone la dumperacha the minute he gets a bad haircut.

Women frequently speak of having had a dreadful relationship just prior to Mr Right's appearance. When you've gone as far along the wrong road as you can go and become thoroughly sick of the view, new turnings, new possibilities miraculously appear.

This is what usually happens when you change your beliefs as investigated in Chapter 12 – you finally come to believe you can have a lovely man and that you deserve love.

Of course, the timing being right necessitates that he wants the same thing too. He's available, he's not giving you mixed messages, or playing any silly relationship games that make chess seem like Hunt the Hippo. He is ready, able and willing to have a relationship with you.

Time will tell

For all the instant recognition and non-dramatic cosying up, it's just the beginning. The only way to really know is to stick it out and see if he still feels like 'The One' two years on. According to anthropologist Helen Fisher, infatuation – lust, passion, call it what you will – only lasts around 18 months. She says: 'We couldn't possibly survive the infatuation zone. We'd die of sexual exhaustion and lack of sleep. Our brains are designed so that after about a year and a half, infatuation wanes, tranquility sets in and attachment takes over.'

So it takes a while to know whether this will go the distance. Professor Clarkson says: 'Many people do recognize someone who looks ideal for them and have a sense of love at first sight, yet often that's based on lust. And when they've gone through that and their lust object has a cold or a bad hair day it all falls apart. Especially for men, love at first sight may be because the woman is the shape of the woman they first loved. Their mother, or a teacher or even a film star of the time. That's not necessarily the real thing, it can be an image. What's different is the love that's both lustful and caring and intelligent, and where you share a life purpose together.'

It's written in the stars

'Life purpose' might sound a little grand, but not to the people who gaze at the stars. To return to Professor Clarkson's question in the 'It's Instant' section (*see page 297*): 'What would possess someone to say yes like that?' An astrologer would reply: He was recognizing destiny. In fact, an astrologer *did* predict she was set to meet her soulmate – not that she believed him – and was only three days out.

Astrology is more than your star sign. That merely tells you where your sun was when you were born. An entire chart plots all the major planets – and the placing of your moon, venus and mars have huge influence on relationships. So when your chart is matched with that of Mr Wonderful, astrologers can often explain why he *is* Mr Wonderful. As Professor Clarkson says: 'My moon was one degree conjunct his sun. That's very rare, apparently, and it's an alchemical marriage.'

When you and your partner have similar planets in similar places you do literally see life the same way, you think and emote in similar ways. This is the astrological evidence for that 'I know you' feeling.

(If you want your chart done contact the Company of Astrologers; or The Astrology Shop in Covent Garden, London.)

And to get even more esoteric for a second, there is a theory in spookland that all our significant relationships are actually with soulmates with whom we have shared past lives. So when you spot your true love and think 'That's him!' you actually *are* recognizing someone who, maybe, was your brother in medieval times, or someone you loved and lost in World War One. There is currently a rash of books on this subject, including Judy Hall's *Hands Across Time – The Soulmate Enigma* (Findhorn Press) or *Only Love is Real – The story of soulmates reunited* by Dr Brian Weiss (Piatkus).

Whether you're intrigued, or whether you think all this is for saddos with a screw loose, when you hook up with Mr Wonderful, it does tend to feel like a date with destiny.

CHAPTER 24

7 Ways Being Single Improves Your Future Relationships

Some of us are becoming the men we wanted to marry.

Gloria Steinham, renowned feminist

Women I talked to for this book were completely convincing on how being single and loving it prepares the ground for true love…

'I'm now a lot more demanding and confident in this present relationship, I'm playing it so casually that he's so desperate he told me he loved me on our second date. It's simply because I don't need him and he knows it. I don't call him, not because I'm a cow but because I don't need him. The only way he'll be with me is if he really really tries.'

Maria, two years single

'The kind of men I went for definitely changed after being single. I had gone very much for public school types – and what do they know about a little Jewish girl from North London? The cultures couldn't be more different. I can't understand someone who's saving for his son to go to Eton before he's even met a woman to have children with. They were all emotionally distant; I was always chasing after someone who was unavailable. But eventually you do get fed up with bad relationships. After a year of being single I met someone who was so certain I was right for him he really pursued me. That was horrific at first – someone who was really nice and really liked me! But he was very persistent and I came to realize it was very nice being with someone who was lovely. So much so I married him.'

Emily, on happy ever after

'Something in me shifted when I was single so that relationships became less all-important. Like the other week I had a huge row on the phone with my boyfriend and I was very upset and cried. And then I went about my business for a couple of days until I saw him again. Of course I thought about it and felt shaken up, but in the past I would have put my life on hold or driven round there in the middle of night because it would have been intolerable. It doesn't mean I don't care, but the cogs have stopped turning that drove my life around a man.'

Kate

'On the train to the party where I met the love of my life I remember thinking I keep dating men who don't have any money. And I felt really pissed off. I was always paying for some young bloke's dinner. So I thought, the next man I date will be able to take me to the River Café (a very posh noshery in London). At the party I noticed this attractive man, and I noticed he found me attractive, and someone asked him what was happening with his big house, and I remember thinking, perhaps he can take me to the River Café. And yes, on our first anniversary, we went there. The unconditional love I'd learnt to have for myself when I was single helps you aim higher.'

Ella

'I used to be a woman who only defined myself by my relationship. From the moment I got my first boyfriend I thought, it's all alright now, I've got someone. Having that someone was more important than anything else. In retrospect it seems a miracle I got any kind of career going at all when I think of the energy I was putting into relationships.

'Then when I was single I started having very real relationships with lots of other people. Like Tina, a great friend I made at art college. She came to meet me on holiday and I had exactly that same buzzy excited in love feeling. Another girlfriend would come and watch Friday night TV every week and all these things felt just as good as doing them with a boyfriend.

'What's interesting is now I'm in a relationship I don't do all those things with my boyfriend. I still do them with my other friends. Now having a relationship with a man is about making love. It's no longer the case that whatever I do with a man is 'special' and the rest of my life isn't. Before, I'd make a big effort when my boyfriend was coming round and buy special food. Now I buy special food anyway and I enjoy it even if it's just me eating it.'

Leah

'I used to say to myself, if I knew that in a year's time I was going to meet someone and everything was going to be great, I'd have a wonderful time now, live life to the full, feel OK about being alone for a bit. So it's that fear that stops you really living life to the full but I've gone through that now. I really do feel I've had a great time – been out loads, done wild things I wouldn't have done otherwise. And things I might not do again. So, when I settle down, especially if I have kids, I'll at least know I've done all the things I wanted first. Now I'll have those memories and know I've done that.'

Jacqui

'When I was on my own I really hit rock bottom. I was so thoroughly once-and-for-all sick of relationships that just weren't right for me. I spent a lot of time alone and though I could never put my hand on my heart and say I preferred it that way it was what was right for me at the time. Then a magical thing happened. Not only did I attract and find myself attracted to someone much nicer, someone who was right for me, but, knowing how much I hated being alone, I appreciate him that much more and I'm more easy going than I was before.'

Rosa

It is the no. 1 challenge: how to be in a relationship and still be yourself, still maintain that ongoing relationship with yourself and not become completely subsumed in coupledom. But if you work with the principles in this book, your relationship will benefit.

In a Relationship and Loving it or Not-Single and Loving it

Here's how the principles of singlehood can transfer to a loving relationship:

1. The relationship is nurturing to you. He looks after you. You look after you.
2. There is room for feelings. His and yours.
3. You get the support you'd get from your girlfriends.
4. You get the fun you'd get from dating.
5. You get to carry on changing and growing as a person.
6. You still have a life outside your relationship. You can still do things on your own.
7. You don't do anything you don't want, even when he wants.
8. You practise your self-awareness. You're also aware of him – you see him clearly, not through rose-tinted spectacles.
9. You're able to assert yourself – be heard, stand up for what you want, and get it.

Summary of part three

In order to be dealing with men again, you are...

- Clear about what/who you are looking for
- Clear you deserve the best
- Looking after yourself on dates when you might be nervous or vulnerable
- Trusting and growing your glorious gut instincts
- Able to say no
- Willing to turn the tables on the old rules and ask someone else out
- Able to take dating destiny into your own hands, maybe even using an outside agency or the Internet
- Determined to get the best for yourself
- Constantly questioning and monitoring how you are in the relationship – and how he is too
- Able to recognize what's right and what's wrong – and act accordingly!

But once we're into the nitty gritty of how to run a relationship, you're not really single any more. So you don't need any more yak from me. You're on your own now, or, rather, you're not. Good luck!